Tenure, Promotion, and Reappointment:
Legal and Administrative Implications

by Benjamin Baez and John A. Centra

ASHE-ERIC Higher Education Report No. 1, 1995

Prepared by

Clearinghouse on Higher Education
The George Washington University

In cooperation with

Association for the Study
of Higher Education

Published by

Graduate School of Education and Human Development
The George Washington University

Jonathan D. Fife, Series Editor

Cite as
Baez, Benjamin, and John A. Centra. 1995. *Tenure, Promotion, and Reappointment: Legal and Administrative Implications*. ASHE-ERIC Higher Education Report No. 1. Washington, D.C.: The George Washington University, School of Education and Human Development.

Library of Congress Catalog Card Number 96-76556
ISSN 0884-0040
ISBN 1-878380-65-6

Managing Editor: Lynne J. Scott
Manuscript Editor: Alexandra Rockey
Cover design by Michael David Brown, Rockville, Maryland

The ERIC Clearinghouse on Higher Educaton invites individuals to submit proposals for writing monographs for the *ASHE-ERIC Higher Education Report* series. Proposals must include:
1. A detailed manuscript proposal of not more than five pages.
2. A chapter-by-chapter outline.
3. A 75-word summary to be used by several review committees for the initial screening and rating of each proposal.
4. A vita and a writing sample.

ERIC Clearinghouse on Higher Education
Graduate School of Education and Human Development
The George Washington University
One Dupont Circle, Suite 630
Washington, DC 20036-1183

This publication was prepared partially with funding from the Office of Education Research and Improvement, U.S. Department of Education, under contract no. ED RR-93-002008. The opinions expressed in this report do not necessarily reflect the positions or policies of OERI or the Department.

EXECUTIVE SUMMARY

Tenure, Promotion, and Reappointment focuses on the legal implications of reappointment, promotion, and tenure decisions, with an emphasis on how understanding the relevant legal principles can inform practice. Through the use of scenarios and cases, we illustrate the conflict between institutional and individual rights and the potential legal problems associated with employment contracts, due process requirements, academic freedom, employment discrimination, affirmative action, and peer review. Suggestions are offered for minimizing litigation and protecting institutional and individual rights. Following are some of the specific questions addressed.

What has been the role of courts in reappointment, promotion, or tenure decisions?

Institutions have a great deal of autonomy and discretion in making reappointment, promotion, or tenure decisions. Courts are reluctant to substitute their judgments for those of academic professionals. Recent legislation permits the submission of employment-discrimination cases to juries, perhaps making it likely that this reluctance may wane. At any rate, courts are required to intervene in these matters when the individual rights of faculty members are threatened. In cases involving discrimination and the First Amendment, courts seem to grant less deference to institutions than in other types of cases.

What is tenure, and why is it the subject of many faculty lawsuits?

Tenure was established to protect faculty members' academic freedom and to provide enough financial security to attract able men and women to the profession. Courts also have established that tenure, once acquired, is a property interest protected by the Constitution when conferred by public institutions. Although cases by faculty members against colleges and universities involve reappointment, promotion, and other issues, the most prominent cases deal with tenure denial. While tenure has benefits for the institution and the faculty members, it also has financial consequences for the institution, especially during times of retrenchment. Faculty members denied tenure suffer financial, professional, and emotional consequences. As a result, lawsuits in this area are likely to increase.

What constitutes the faculty employment contract?

The faculty contract of employment refers not only to the letter of appointment but to other professional and institutional policies governing reappointment, promotion, and tenure decisions. Institutional policies are included in the faculty handbook, while American Association of University Professors policy statements, especially the 1940 Statement of Principles on Academic Freedom and Tenure, contain professional policies. Courts also have looked to institutional practices and customs and the oral, written, and implied assurances of key administrators to determine the rights and responsibilities of the parties when the language of the contract is unclear, ambiguous, or inconsistent. Collective-bargaining agreements are important types of contracts, and they may govern how faculty members are reappointed, promoted, or tenured. Federal labor law, which governs private collective bargaining, excludes faculty members who are considered "managers" and/or "supervisors," and thus institutions may refuse to bargain with their representatives. Faculty members are more likely to be considered "managers" or "supervisors" at large, private research institutions. Faculty members at public institutions also may be restricted in the collective-bargaining ability under their states' labor laws. Collective bargaining is an extremely complex and unsettled area of law, and institutions should seek expert legal and administrative assistance in dealing with such matters.

To what extent are untenured faculty members at public institutions entitled to due process under the Constitution?

The Constitution protects the property interests of faculty members at public institutions. Before such interests may be denied or withheld, public institutions must provide their faculty members with due process protection, including adequate notice and a hearing. Untenured faculty members at public institutions have due process rights for the duration of their contracts, but not after the contract expires — unless the contract of employment or state law provides them with a legitimate expectation of continued employment. Some faculty members may contend that they have acquired tenure informally. Courts usually are unwilling to find that faculty members have acquired tenure through informal means, especially if there are written and explicit policies governing how tenure is acquired. All faculty members at public institutions are entitled to due process protection when their liberty interests are arguably infringed. Liberty interests arise when institutions make charges or allegations against faculty members that may damage their reputations or impose a "stigma or other disability" preventing them from obtaining other employment. In negative reappointment, promotion, or tenure decisions, liberty interests are difficult to prove because the reasons for the denial rarely are made public, a required condition for prevailing in such a lawsuit.

How do courts balance institutional and individual academic freedom rights?

Institutions have the freedom to decide on academic grounds who may teach, what may be taught, how it shall be taught, and who may be admitted to study. As a result, courts are reluctant to become involved in academic matters such as pedagogy, grading, and course offerings unless the institutions' decisions are intended to punish faculty members for their speech. Courts will become involved in negative employment decisions at public institutions that are motivated by the faculty members' exercise of their First Amendment or academic freedom rights. These rights include the freedom to comment on matters of public concern, the freedom to speak and express oneself even if such speech is considered offensive, and the freedom to engage in certain activities such as testifying in court cases or engaging in political or union activities.

How are faculty members protected from illegal discrimination in reappointment, promotion, or tenure decisions?

Although the Constitution and state laws prohibit discrimination, the bulk of the employment-discrimination litigation has involved a number of federal civil-rights laws, especially Title VII of the Civil Rights Act of 1964. Federal civil-rights laws provide an easier burden of proof for faculty members alleging illegal discrimination than does the Constitution. These laws also provide better guidance to institutions for avoiding discrimination than many state laws. Given the inherent subjectivity of the promotion and tenure process, what is considered fair or meritorious is difficult to determine and will vary from person to person. Furthermore, some policies or practices adversely affect women and faculty of color. As a result, employment-discrimination cases have been increasing, and colleges and universities should justify their reappointment, promotion, and tenure decisions with clear data and careful documentation.

What are the legal boundaries of affirmative action in faculty employment?

Affirmative action in the reappointment, promotion, and tenure process seeks to accomplish three objectives: eliminate the effects of an institution's own present or prior discrimination against women and people of color; remedy societal discrimination and increase the representation of women and people of color in the faculty ranks; and promote racial and gender diversity on college campuses. But as the current societal and political debate makes clear, faculty members who do not benefit from affirmative action may believe that their individual rights have been violated and that they have been the victims of reverse discrimination. Institutions of higher education may believe that a balance between the goals of affirmative action and claims of reverse discrimination is impossible to attain.

Nevertheless, institutions have been able to justify affirmative action if they are attempting to remedy the effects of their own discrimination. In addition, Title VII permits private and public institutions to implement voluntary affirmative-action plans if there is a "manifest imbalance" in the job market, if the plans are only temporary, and if the interests of faculty members not benefiting from affirmative action are not unnecessarily "trammeled." Public institutions, however, are subject to much stronger standards of justification on constitutional grounds.

What rights do faculty members have to access confidential peer-review materials?

Faculty members or the EEOC may be able to obtain access to peer-review materials to discover proof of discrimination. Furthermore, in some states, peer evaluations are made generally available to faculty members under employee "right to know" or "sunshine" laws. Although faculty members alleging discrimination have been given access to their and others' personnel files, courts have been generally concerned with the impact this disclosure has on the peer-review process. As a result, courts continue to search for a balance between the importance of confidentiality for the peer-review system and the need to prohibit discrimination in higher education.

The peer-review system likely will not suffer from disclosure of confidential peer-review materials. Peer evaluations based upon sound and fair reasoning will always withstand challenges. Even though courts will compel disclosure in some situations, the decision of whether to voluntarily release peer-review materials to the faculty member is one of institutional policy. Some institutions provide faculty members with, at a minimum, a redacted (with identifying information deleted, for example) copy of the peer-review materials, and recent data indicate that the peer-review system is not greatly affected by disclosure of peer-review materials.

To what extent are administrators and faculty members involved in the peer-review process liable for defamation and other tort claims?

Although faculty members and administrators involved in the peer-review process can be sued for defamation and other torts, they usually are protected from liability by state law, or a qualified privilege*. Also, most institutions have insurance covering this type of matter. Peer reviewers can lose this protection if they act with malice or bad faith or disclose the information to people who have no legitimate interest in the matter. As long as they act honestly and fairly and provide detailed examples for their conclusions, administrators and faculty members involved in the peer-review process generally are protected from liability.

What can we do to minimize the risk of litigation?

Administrators, faculty members, and institutional attorneys should function as a team in informing other administrators and faculty members about the legal implications of their responsibilities. Legal audits should be performed periodi-

---

*Qualified privileges against liability from defamation and other torts are granted to people making employment evaluations, provided they acted without malice or ill will. The law grants these privileges when the interests at stake warrant them.

cally. These legal audits involve surveying each office and function to ensure that policies and practices are in compliance with legal principles. Furthermore, legal audits and teamwork can serve as an early warning system that alerts administrators, faculty members, and legal counsel of potential legal problems long before they lead to litigation. Institutions should take steps to minimize the risks from litigation. We recommend the following:

- Institutions should involve legal counsel in determining policy and procedures for reappointment, promotion, and tenure decisions.
- The reappointment, promotion, and tenure policies should be explicit, unambiguous, and consistent, and these policies should clearly articulate how tenure is to be acquired.
- Institutions should eliminate or minimize those practices that are not specifically addressed in the institutions' written policies.
- Institutional officers and key administrators should be informed that their actions and words can bind the institutions to a contract.
- All units in the institution should be governed by a single reappointment, promotion, and tenure policy, though the standards may differ among units.
- The criteria for reappointment, promotion, or tenure should be specific enough to provide guidance to faculty members.
- Faculty members should be provided with as much information as possible as they prepare for their reappointment, promotion, or tenure review.
- Faculty members should be provided procedural safeguards before they are released from their contracts.
- Institutions should provide orientation and career development for new faculty members.
- Institutions should develop a process of annually evaluating faculty members.
- The faculty member should be apprised of any performance problem with enough time to improve.
- Faculty members should be provided with, at the very least, a redacted copy of their performance evaluations and peer-review materials.
- Institutions should commit themselves to ending discrimi-

nation and to take whatever steps are necessary to achieve this end.

- Institutions should be conscious of the important legal, political, and social interests associated with affirmative action.
- Individuals involved in the evaluation or review process must be made aware of the fundamentals of employment-discrimination law.
- Institutions should establish grievance procedures that are easy to use.
- Institutions should consider adopting binding arbitration or another method of alternative dispute resolution.

CONTENTS

FOREWORD

The fear of every college president or dean is to see the newspaper headline: **PROFESSOR AWARDED $3 MILLION IN PERSONNEL SUIT.** This fear seems to be justified because personnel matters are the single largest area of litigation for institutions. Institutions need to protect their scarce resources from being redirected from the pursuit of their academic mission.

It should be understood that faculty do not sue their institutions on a whim. There are always reasons, real or imagined, that cause an individual to enter into an adversarial relationship with the organization he or she once joined voluntarily with the hopes of a productive lifetime career. The major causes of faculty litigation are:

- **Poor training:** On the whole, key academic leaders, from academic vice presidents to department chairs, have not been instructed on the motives underlying most personnel disputes. As a consequence of this unknowingness, these key institutional leaders may respond in manner which puts the institution at risk.
- **Violation of written agreements:** The first area of concern to the courts is that once an agreement is made, it is faithfully executed. Most faculty disputes occur because the institution has failed to uphold its agreement with the individual. This agreement could be found as part of the faculty contract or could be part of the policies that govern the institution, e.g., faculty code or personnel procedures.
- **Violation of basic rights:** The second area of concern to the courts is that the rights of the individual be protected from the oppression of governmental agencies or impersonal organizations. These basic rights are detailed in federal and state constitutions and in the various non-discrimination federal regulations.
- **Inconsistent enforcement of procedures:** One concept of nondiscrimination is that everyone is treated the same. Therefore, policies and procedures that are applied inconsistently are considered by the courts to be inherently unacceptable.
- **Faculty perception of being treated unfairly:** Poor communication and a sense of not being appreciated may be all it takes to motivate a faculty member to sue.

Litigation of this type may be few in number, but it does take up a significant percentage of the time spent by the college counsel.

Academic leaders must develop policies and practices that are sensitive to the changing needs of the institution. The changes higher education has experienced in the knowledge base, financial issues, expectations of students, and demands by society have increased significantly during the past 20 years and are accelerating. Balancing the needs of rapid change while protecting the rights and expectations of faculty will take increasing skill.

In this report, Benjamin Baez, an instructor of higher education at Syracuse University, and John A. Centra, professor and chairman of the Higher Education program at Syracuse University, have developed a comprehensive view of faculty legal issues concerning tenure, promotion and reappointments. They address the primary areas of litigation: contracts; constitutional law—including due process rights; freedom of speech and academic freedom considerations; employment discrimination; affirmative action, including diversity and individual rights; and peer review. Baez and Centra have provided an analysis that will be extremely useful for institutions to begin a comprehensive legal-education program for their academic leadership.

When an institution establishes such a training program, the benefits will include an awareness of the legal implications of individual acts, development of a sensitivity to the need to consistently enforce the policies and procedures of the institution, and development of a stronger relationship between the actions of individuals to the overall mission of the institution. The end result is the development of a culture that is more nurturing and supportive of faculty rights, more consistent with the academic purpose of the institution, and more protective of individuals with less power and influence. In short, a leadership that has a firmer foundation regarding its legal rights and responsibilities and better able to create a culture of trust that fosters an attitude of appreciation rather than an attitude of mistrust protected by a shield of litigation.

Jonathan D. Fife
Series Editor, Professor of Higher Education Administration, and
Director, ERIC Clearinghouse on Higher Education

ACKNOWLEDGMENTS

This report is dedicated to faculty members, especially those who were unsuccessful in their bid to attain tenure. Even though many faculty members do not, and many will not, attain promotion and tenure, we all can learn from their efforts. The faculty members and institutions that are the subjects of the cases discussed in this report may or may not have won their lawsuits, but they have provided us with lessons that can help us ensure fairness during these particularly stressful but essential processes.

We would like to thank our spouses, Rochelle Parnes and Nancy Centra, for their support and patience during the writing of this manuscript and the performance of our other responsibilities. Furthermore, we extend our thanks to the four anonymous reviewers for their assistance in identifying important sources and providing insightful feedback and suggestions.

INTRODUCTION: TENURE IN AMERICAN HIGHER EDUCATION

This report addresses the rights and limitations of faculty members and institutions in reappointment, promotion, and tenure decisions. Although colleges and universities have a great deal of discretion and autonomy from court intervention in employment matters, they also confront legal limitations. The following sections explore broad questions with regard to negative reappointment, promotion, and tenure decisions:

- What rights and responsibilities do institutions and faculty members have under the employment contract?
- Are untenured faculty members entitled to constitutional due process?
- How are the academic freedoms of the institution and faculty members balanced?
- What protection do faculty members have against illegal discrimination?
- What rights do faculty members have to inspect peer-review information?
- What are the legal boundaries of affirmative action?
- What can we learn from the exploration of these issues that would help administrators and faculty members make legal and fair decisions?

This report addresses the rights and limitations of faculty members and institutions in reappointment, promotion, and tenure decisions.

Tenure in American Higher Education

Although this report addresses the legal implications of reappointment, promotion, and tenure decisions, tenure is the crux of the discussion and the subject of many lawsuits involving faculty members. Tenure in American higher education has a long and varied history. As defined by the American Association of University Professors, or AAUP, 1940 Statement of Principles on Academic Freedom and Tenure, which has been adopted by many, if not most, institutions and is relied upon by many state and federal courts, tenure protects a faculty member's freedom to teach, research, and engage in extramural activities, and it provides sufficient economic security to make the academic profession attractive to able men and women (AAUP 1990). Although tenure does not guarantee lifetime employment, dismissal becomes very difficult once a faculty member has attained tenure.

Tenure has been criticized widely within higher education as well as outside (*Wall Street Journal*, Oct. 10, 1994). As a result, many in higher education argued that the tenure system should be reformed (Trachtenberg, January/February 1996). The American Association for Higher Education began a two-year project examining tenure (*Chronicle of Higher Education*, March 31, 1995). Of course, many professors and presidents defend the intent, if not the alleged abuses, of the American tenure system (Cotter, January/February 1996).

Tenure does not come without costs to an institution. In addition to the risks that the tenured professor may become an ineffective teacher, stop publishing, and be a poor citizen, there are other costs. Financially, the employing institution commits to a potential lifetime appointment that may cost it approximately $2 million by the time the tenured professor retires (Brown and Kurland 1993). In response to these criticisms, opponents have called for an elimination or modification of tenure. Some institutions have adopted alternatives to tenure by employing faculty members on term contracts; others have modified their tenure system by enacting nontenure track appointments, extended probationary periods, suspension of the "up-or-out" rule, imposition of tenure quotas, and periodic evaluation of tenured faculty members (Chait and Ford 1982).

There are benefits for the institution and the faculty member. The faculty member is rewarded for his or her work and gains job security. For the institution, the American tenure system, with its "up-or-out" policy, does not allow marginal professors, though popular, to linger on. Tenure also is a trade-off for the lower salaries paid to faculty members compared with other professionals; certainly, the lack of job security generally would require higher salaries (Brown and Kurland 1993; Franke 1995). Given the lower salaries, academic institutions are able to recruit quality professors with the promise of tenure.

But most importantly, tenure protects and enhances academic freedom (Commission on Academic Tenure in Higher Education 1973; Olswang and Lee 1984). Professors can be assured of performing their responsibilities without interference or fear of losing their jobs. Job security promotes academic freedom by encouraging innovation and commitment to long-term projects. Furthermore, because senior faculty members do not feel professionally threatened by bringing in men and women of ability, they maintain the quality of the institution's faculty (Brown and Kurland 1993).

Tenure policies and procedures

Tenure is the central feature of academic staffing policies in most colleges and universities; approximately 85 percent of all colleges and universities have tenure systems (Mortimer, Bagshaw, and Masland 1985). Some institutions, however — most of them junior and community colleges — do not. These institutions instead operate under some form of a contract system.

Most institutions of higher education have rules and regulations regarding the review of probationary faculty. Faculty members are reviewed to determine whether they meet the scholarly and instructional standards justifying tenure awards. Such evaluation traditionally has been vested in the faculty. This practice is consistent with AAUP principles, and the courts generally have viewed faculty as the most appropriate evaluators of academic merit (Olswang and Lee 1984).

The 1940 Statement of Principles, although almost universally endorsed and adopted, does not prescribe institutional practice; it merely offers guidance. As a result, promotion and tenure policies and practices differ greatly from institution to institution and sometimes within institutional units and departments. Every aspect of tenure may differ: the definition; the criteria for awards; the length of the probationary period; categories of eligible faculty members; the relationship between tenure and rank; the procedures for recommending; the procedures for appealing adverse decisions; the role of faculty, administration, students, and governing boards in these decisions; and the methods of evaluating teaching, scholarship, and service — the most common criteria for promotion and tenure.

A study by the Commission on Academic Tenure in Higher Education highlighted the variability in promotion and tenure policies and practices (1973). This variability is still true today. While most colleges and universities have formal tenure policies and procedures, some do not. Most institutions provide explicit statements concerning the qualifications and criteria for reappointment, promotion, and tenure, although some do not. Increasingly, efforts are made to assist the young faculty member in developing as teacher and scholar, but in some colleges and universities the young faculty member still is given virtually no assistance or information about his or her strengths or shortcomings until the tenure decision is made. Institutions may evaluate their faculty member annually, every three years, or only once (when the tenure decision is made).

Some colleges and universities limit the proportion of tenured faculty in a given department, but most do not have specific limitations. Often, the tenure decisions start with and generally follow the recommendations of departmental committees, but at some institutions the departmental chairperson or dean makes the effective recommendation, with or without formal faculty consultation. At many institutions the board of trustees makes the final decisions, although at some colleges presidents or other principal academic officers have the ultimate authority to grant tenure. Many institutions also have grievance procedures that allow faculty members to appeal unfavorable tenure decisions, although a few colleges and universities do not.

Despite the variability, some commonalities exist. Usually, faculty members reach the tenure decision after some period of probationary service that commonly ranges from three to seven years, averaging six years at universities and five and one-half years at four-year colleges (Chait and Ford 1982). The review process typically lasts for most of the academic year and involves input from peer-review committees, department heads, deans, and other administrators (Leap 1993). The faculty member is burdened with proving his or her worthiness; should the decision be negative, the faculty member is given a one-year terminal contract. In institutions that permit promotion before the tenure decision is made, the faculty member denied promotion likely will not receive tenure.

Peer-review committees, normally consisting of departmental colleagues, typically make the initial recommendation on reappointment, promotion, or tenure. Once these committees have made their recommendations, the dossier is forwarded to the department head and then the college dean (in many cases, the department head sees the dossier first). The recommendations of the committees, department head, or dean usually are not binding but often are followed. The dossier then is forwarded to the chief academic officer and then the college president. These administrators, for all practical purposes, hold the final authority to grant or deny tenure because the governing boards (which often have the legal authority) usually rubber stamp these decisions (see Leap 1993; Whicker, Kronenfeld, and Strickland 1993). There have been instances, however, in which a governing board has denied tenure despite the recommendations of these administrators. For example, the board of trustees for the University of Massachusetts System recently denied tenure to three professors whose promotions had been approved by campus and system officials. A board subcommittee was concerned about the proportion of tenured professors in the system (*Chronicle of Higher Education*, Sept. 8, 1995).

The primary criteria for promotion and tenure decisions are teaching effectiveness, research and publications, and service to the public, profession, and the institution. But how these criteria are measured and weighed varies from institution to institution (Diamond 1994; Kogan, Moses, and El-Khawas 1994; Leap 1993). Although institutions vary in the methods they use to evaluate faculty, there has been a significant increase in the use of student evaluations, and more recently teaching portfolios, for summative evaluation of faculty members (Centra 1993). The institutions also may consider such institutional needs as financial constraints, departmental growth or decline, and curricular or program changes (Diamond 1994; Leap 1993). Faculty members usually are required to submit a dossier that illustrates and summarizes their accomplishments, as well as other documents (such as letters of reference). Institutions also seek letters of evaluations from scholars at other institutions (Leap 1993).

Given the financial constraints that most institutions observe, many faculty members will not achieve tenure; many will be hired on nontenure tracks and others will not be granted tenure because of the already high percentage of tenured faculty at many colleges and universities (Brooks and German 1983; *Chronicle of Higher Education*, Sept. 8, 1995). Because of the benefits of tenure, the subjective nature of the procedures and criteria, and the drastic consequences of a negative promotion and tenure decision, faculty members sometimes will choose to seek a judicial remedy in a state or federal court. We are likely to see more faculty members seeking remedy in the courts.

Tenure, furthermore, does not guarantee lifetime employment. This also is true in public institutions in which tenure attainment gives faculty members a "property interest" protected by the due process clause of the 14th Amendment. Tenure only protects a faculty member from being dismissed without cause, although an institution is required to provide faculty members with adequate notice and a hearing before dismissal. Many courts have upheld dismissal of tenured faculty members for, among other reasons, incompetence (*Riggin vs. Board of Trustees of Ball State University* 1986), sexual or "unprofessional" misconduct (*Korf vs. Ball State University* 1984), neglect of duties (*King vs. University of Minnesota* 1985), financial exigency (*Krotkoff vs. Goucher College* 1978), and program discontinuance (*Jimenez vs. Almodovar* 1981).

Although many institutions do not have systematic reviews of tenured faculty, some scholars have called for periodic evaluation of tenured faculty members (Olswang and Fantel 1980). Certain professional trends suggest that tenured faculty members may be required to submit to more strenuous review procedures: the demands for quality, increased interest in periodic review of tenured faculty, elimination of mandatory retirement, and the obligation to end sexual harassment (Moll 1992). Furthermore, given the backlash against tenure and increased financial difficulties at many colleges and universities, more institutions may begin to question the perceived tradition of maintaining tenured professors who do not perform adequately or engage in unprofessional conduct.

History of Tenure and Promotion

Tenure as we know it today, with a set of due process rights that go with its acquisition, did not exist prior to the 1940s (Metzger 1993a). In the 19th century, many institutions appointed their faculty for one year, vacated their positions at the end of the term, and reappointed only those who passed the annual review (Metzger 1973). This practice was most common in state-supported institutions and was justified by governing boards on the grounds that yearly appropriations made it difficult to commit to long-term appointments. Furthermore, if indefinite tenure existed at all, the law treated it as temporary and extinguishable (Metzger 1973).

Since professors had indicated concern about their job security and many of them sought freedom for their expressions and beliefs, the AAUP, born in 1915, issued a declaration of general principles on tenure and academic freedom (Metzger 1973). The AAUP sought to accomplish two goals:

the right to establish the faculty as the body best able to judge the qualifications of other faculty, and the use of certain procedures (such as written charges and a faculty trial) to make it more difficult for the institution to dismiss faculty members capriciously.

Before the 1940s, some institutions gave tenure (that is, continued appointment without explicit renewal) to faculty members at the rank of full or associate professor, while others did not give tenure at all. In institutions with tenure, the lower floor was turned into a "proving ground from which qualified persons could be lifted out of insecurity on the elevator of promotion" (Metzger 1993a). Most of the institutions, however, did not set a limit on the number of times short-term appointments could be renewed, and so some teachers could compile many years of service without ever gaining tenure. The AAUP addressed some of these concerns in 1940.

The 1940 Statement of Principles on Academic Freedom and Tenure was issued jointly by the AAUP and the Association of American Colleges. Over the years, the 1940 Statement of Principles has been incorporated expressly or by reference into many faculty handbooks, endorsed by more than 100 national learned and professional associations, and relied upon by a number of courts; it is the general norm of academic practice in American higher education (Van Alstyne 1993b).

The 1940 Statement of Principles emphasized job security. By its use of the word "probationary" to describe the pre-tenure service, it made it clear that this pre-tenure period could not be used as a form of "cheap labor." The statement also disengaged tenure from rank and tied it to years of service, which was reckoned as all the years spent in the profession. De facto tenure (or tenure accrued by nonformal means rather than institutional say-so) thereby became possible (Metzger 1973). The 1940 Statement of Principles also required that the dismissal of tenured professors could only be accomplished by showing financial exigency or cause.

The 1940 Statement of Principles protected tenured faculty members. The AAUP, in response to the dismissal of untenured professors during the McCarthy era, called for the procedural protection of these faculty members (Brown and Kurland 1993). The AAUP safeguards include hearings when violations of academic freedom are alleged and sufficient notice of nonreappointment so that a faculty member has time to relocate or to seek reconsideration of the negative decision.

Legal history of tenure and promotion

The courts in the early 1900s tended to view colleges and universities as just another kind of corporation, and the early academic-employment cases indicated extensive judicial deference to academic decisionmakers as long as there was a showing that the termination of appointments were in the best interests of an institution (Olswang and Lee 1984). The Supreme Court, however, moved toward recognizing academic freedom (which was protected by tenure) as a legitimate constitutional value in *Sweezy vs. New Hampshire* (1957). This decision overturned a contempt conviction of a professor who refused to disclose what he discussed in a class lecture (Van Alstyne 1993b). In *Keyishian vs. Board of Regents* (1967), the Supreme Court eliminated all but the most general loyalty oaths and recognized that academic freedom is a "special concern" of the First Amendment. In addition to freedom to engage in political speech, courts also have recognized the freedom of faculty members to engage in teaching and other classroom activities, as well as the freedom to conduct research (Olswang and Lee 1984).

In later cases, the Supreme Court established tenure at public institutions, once acquired, as a "property interest," protected by the due process clause of the 14th Amendment (see Section Three). Tenure rights may be governed by the employment contract or state law, but once acquired public institutions must establish extremely good reasons (and provide proper procedural safeguards) before dismissing a tenured faculty member.

Untenured faculty members, on the other hand, are not protected by the Constitution after their contracts have expired*. Their rights for nonrenewal are primarily established by the employment contract, which may protect them by providing grievance procedures and other safeguards. Untenured faculty members also may have rights under state law. Tenure plans at public institutions, for example, may be

---

*Untenured faculty members are protected while their contracts are in effect, but nonrenewal is not a deprivation of property interest (*Board of Regents vs. Roth* 1972).

governed by state law, and any decision contrary to these plans may result in litigation and, in rare cases, the judicially mandated tenure of these faculty members.

The AAUP definition of academic freedom and tenure emphasizes the protection of individual professors against the institution, whereas the constitutional definition seems to emphasize the protection of the individual and the entire university community against state intervention (Rabban 1993). The freedom to determine who may teach, what may be taught, and how it shall be taught apparently covers the appointment, promotion, tenure, and the elimination of faculty, as well as curriculum issues, pedagogy, and student admissions (Rabban 1993).

The AAUP's definition of academic freedom is important because courts have used it to establish the employment rights of professors whose appointments have been terminated. When the institution has incorporated this definition into faculty handbooks or other documents, courts have determined that it is part of the employment contract* (see *Greene vs. Howard University* 1969; Olswang and Lee 1984). Even when institutions have not explicitly incorporated the AAUP definition into their policy documents, courts may hold that institutions are responsible for complying with these principles, interpreting them as a kind of "industry practice" (Olswang and Lee 1984).

To grasp the legal implications of reappointment, promotion, and tenure decisions, it is important to understand how courts view the faculty-institution relationship.

The Nature of the Faculty-Institution Relationship

To grasp the legal implications of reappointment, promotion, and tenure decisions, it is important to understand how courts view the faculty-institution relationship. This relationship is primarily defined by contract law, but certain issues are resolved by labor law, employment-discrimination law, and, in public institutions, constitutional law and public employment statutes and regulations (Kaplin and Lee 1995). Since the Constitution provides safeguards against state action, private institutions rarely are subject to the constitutional requirements imposed on public institutions (via the 14th Amendment, for example). Therefore, contract law provides the primary basis for defining the rights of private institutions and their faculty.

---

*While most states treat faculty handbooks as contracts, a few still do not.

The legal implications of promotion and tenure decisions

Given the importance of promotion and tenure decisions to the institution and individual faculty members and the legal history established, resorting to the courts for a remedy is not unusual. Faculty-employment decisions account for the greatest proportion of litigation against colleges and universities (Lee 1985). This is not surprising. Financial constraints in higher education have decreased the number of faculty positions. The high number of tenured faculty and the financial costs associated with tenure have forced many institutions to toughen the standards for granting promotion and tenure, leading to more negative decisions in a tighter job market. And employment-discrimination laws provide more channels for challenging negative decisions (Lee 1985).

Though courts often defer to academic expertise in employment matters, an institution may not violate a faculty member's civil, constitutional (at public institutions), or contractual rights. Courts will look to the facts of a case to determine whether the stated reasons for denying promotion or tenure are impermissible or whether there was a substantial departure from accepted "academic norms" (Rabban 1993). The role of the courts, however, is not to review and correct mistakes but to ensure that the decisions are consistent with legal requirements. As a result of this limited view, most legal claims by individual faculty members have been rejected (Rabban 1993).

Despite all the concern by administrators and faculty members about the competence of judges to evaluate subjective employment decisions, courts rarely question substantive decisions (Lee 1985). And when they have looked into these decisions, they have focused on factors not unique to academia — namely, the timing of the decisions and quantifiable data (Rabban 1993).

Nevertheless, courts sometimes have reviewed the substance of these decisions to determine whether faculty members' rights were violated. This is especially true in discrimination and First Amendment cases. In a number of cases in which the reasons for a negative employment decision have been considered weak or poorly substantiated or where the unanimous decision of the faculty committees was overturned by upper-level administrators, the courts have found that the stated academic reasons were a pretext for an illegal decision (Rabban 1993).

The Use of Scenarios

Because we believe that complex legal issues are best understood when specific problems are at issue, this report uses scenarios to guide the readers through the issues discussed in each section. For this reason, we also provide a more extensive discussion of the facts of cases then one might see in reports dealing with legal issues. These scenarios are composites of actual cases and provide the readers with realistic examples of how these legal issues might manifest in practice. Each section begins with a scenario or two and some questions about scenario(s). At the end of the section and after we have discussed the relevant legal doctrines, we return to the scenario and provide possible answers to these questions. Readers may choose to return to the scenario to refresh their memories before reading our answers.

Summary

Institutions have a great deal of autonomy and discretion in making reappointment, promotion, or tenure decisions. Courts are reluctant to substitute their judgments for those of academic professionals. On the other hand, courts are required to intervene in these matters when the individual rights of faculty members are threatened. Although cases by faculty members against colleges and universities involve reappointment, promotion, and other issues, the most important cases deal with tenure denial. Tenure has many benefits for institutions and faculty members, but it also has financial consequences for the institution. The financial, professional, and emotional consequences of a negative tenure decision for faculty members likely will result in many more such lawsuits.

THE FACULTY CONTRACT OF EMPLOYMENT

Consider these scenarios:

The faculty handbook at XYZ College, a private institution, states that "full-time faculty members are entitled to tenure at the end of their seventh year of service, provided they have proven merit in teaching, scholarship, and service." Faculty members must apply for tenure in their sixth year, and the handbook describes the process. Professor A, a male faculty member in the English department, served as an adjunct professor for two academic years teaching three classes each semester before being appointed assistant professor Aug. 1, 1990, on annual contracts.

On Aug. 1, 1994, Professor A was informed that as of July 30, 1995, his services no longer would be required. The college was not "dissatisfied" with Professor A's performance, but it was experiencing financial difficulties. As a result, it was eliminating positions in a number of departments. Professor A claimed that pursuant to the handbook, the completion of his last year automatically gives him tenure. He also contended that since he has served the college for six full years, at the very least he should be permitted to apply for tenure. The college argued that no faculty member is "entitled" to tenure, and only full-time faculty members are eligible to apply for tenure at the start of their sixth year. Since Professor A was notified of dismissal before his sixth year, he is not eligible for tenure. The tenure policies do not address the issue of adjunct professors. Professor A claimed that his department chairperson indicated to him that his two years as adjunct would be considered "full time."

In addition to Professor A's position, XYZ College eliminated a number of other untenured faculty positions for financial reasons. Many faculty members disagreed that the college was motivated by legitimate financial reasons. Many of them also believed they had little say about the elimination of faculty positions. As a result, a number of tenured and untenured faculty members met to discuss whether it would be appropriate to form a union to bargain collectively with the college regarding when and how faculty should be dismissed and other employment matters.

On paper, the administration retains ultimate decision-making authority in all matters. The faculty at XYZ College, however, have almost unfettered autonomy about curriculum issues, admission and graduation standards, and grading policies. The faculty also provide recommendations about hiring, promotion, and tenure matters, and although the administration usually accepts these recommendations, it has overturned their recommendations in some cases. The administration also seeks faculty input into many other decisions, and faculty members often are represented in internal committees that make recommendations to the administration on many matters.

Does Professor A have tenure? At the very least, should he be permitted to apply for tenure? Are the faculty members able to bargain collectively with the college? These questions will be addressed at the end of this section.

Traditionally, employment relationships have been considered "at will," meaning that either party may terminate the relationship at any time for any legal reason. In higher education, however, the concept of "employment at will" is not appropriate to describe the faculty-institution relationship. Administrators and clerical and support staff members may be "at will" employees, but faculty members rarely are. For one, tenure has made the faculty-institution relationship distinct from that of other professions. Tenure protects faculty members from dismissal without cause. Untenured faculty members also are not "at will" employees. They usually have term contracts — typically for one year — although these contracts may be longer at some institutions. These faculty members are protected from dismissal for any reason for the duration of their contract periods.

But untenured faculty members have no rights after the expiration of their contracts, and both parties may end their employment relationship, for any reason, without subjecting themselves to any legal obligations. Increasingly, untenured faculty members are attempting to seek rights beyond the terms of their contracts, usually asserting that verbal (that is, oral or written) assurances or promises, academic custom or practice, and/or institutional policy statements ensured them continual employment (Hustoles 1983). It is this issue (the

attempt to extend their rights beyond the terms of the contract) that is the focus of this section.

The contract of employment is the primary basis for
determining the rights and obligations of faculty members
and their institutions regarding reappointment, promotion,
or tenure decisions. The employment contract can include
the notice of appointment, institutional policy statements,
and other documents, including the 1940 Statement of
Principles. Since courts may look to all these materials to
resolve contractual disputes, administrators should exercise
care in drafting and implementing these documents. Failure
to carefully draft these materials may lead to expensive lawsuits, legal remedies for the faculty member, and in some
rare cases the possibility of judicially imposed reappointment, promotion, or tenure of a faculty member. One of the
most complex and unsettled legal areas in contract law is
collective bargaining; administrators and faculty members
seeking to understand their rights and obligations under a
collective-bargaining agreement are advised to seek special
legal and administrative assistance.

1940 Statement of Principles and Other AAUP Policy Statements

The 1940 Statement of Principles is extremely important in
the area of faculty employment. The statement has been
incorporated expressly or by reference into many faculty
handbooks (Van Alstyne 1993b). In many cases, where the
contract of employment was unclear or ambiguous, courts
have looked to the 1940 Statement of Principles as evidence
of academic custom.

The 1940 Statement of Principles states that:

> *After the expiration of a probationary period, teachers or
> investigators should have permanent or continuous
> tenure, and their service should be terminated only for
> adequate cause, except in the case of retirement for age,
> or under extraordinary circumstances because of finan-
> cial exigencies* (AAUP 1990).

The 1940 Statement of Principles is directly responsible for
the "up or out" rule by providing that "acceptable academic
practice" requires that the probationary period should not be
longer than seven years, including prior service at other

institutions. This policy applies to all full-time faculty members regardless of rank and credentials, and an institution's attempt to increase the length of the probationary period would run contrary to this policy. The probation period ensures that institutions do not take advantage of faculty members by keeping them in vulnerable positions indefinitely. Some institutions, for example, increase the probationary period by placing new faculty members who have not completed the terminal degree in a "pre-probationary" status, not starting the "tenure clock" until the degree is attained. In a strict sense, even this practice runs counter to the 1940 Statement of Principles.

Not all extensions, however, hurt faculty members. For example, many institutions give faculty members the option of claiming prior service at another institution toward the probationary period; this may extend the probationary period, allowing these faculty members more time to attain tenure. Also, some institutions have tenure policies that allow any parent of a newborn extra time to earn tenure, although women are particularly vulnerable to the "up-or-out" rule. The current practice of proving oneself within six years has forced many women to choose between their careers and parenthood or to delay having children until their late thirties or early forties (*Chronicle of Higher Education*, March 10, 1995). In some cases, women have lost their jobs because they have chosen to have children during their probationary period, minimizing their productivity.

Although available at many institutions, extensions granted for rearing children are controversial to some critics. Institutions that permit these extensions may find it more difficult to refuse them to those who need to complete their doctoral degrees or who were saddled with prior service elsewhere (although many institutions do count some prior service and do not force the faculty member to complete another seven years). Some argue that extensions of the seven-year probationary period, even when a faculty member has served at another institution, may undermine the tenure system and weaken its protection of academic freedom (see Brown and Kurland 1993). The AAUP realized that legitimate needs exist justifying an extension of the probationary period and modified its policy in 1978 by acknowledging that when faculty members move to another institution, it may be in the best interests of both parties to determine at the time of initial appointment whether to delay the tenure decision beyond the seven-year period required by the 1940 Statement of Principles (Brown and Kurland 1993).

Institutions that have incorporated the 1940 Statement of Principles, or any other AAUP policy statement, into their employment contracts or faculty handbooks have been required to uphold its tenets. As mentioned previously, even if an institution has not explicitly incorporated the 1940 Statement of Principles into its employment contracts, courts sometimes have held institutions responsible for complying with the statement, viewing it as evidence of "industry practice" based on widely held norms and beliefs (Olswang and Lee 1984, p. 9). This does not mean, however, that faculty members will always prevail in court. In *Hill vs. Talledega College* (1987), three faculty members appointed on one-year contracts in August 1984 were informed by letter in May 1985 that their services no longer would be required. Each faculty member filed a separate lawsuit, alleging that the college failed to apply the AAUP's Procedural Standards in Faculty Dismissals Proceedings, which provides elaborate procedural standards that must be followed before a faculty member can be dismissed. The court consolidated the three cases because they essentially dealt with the same claims. Without deciding whether this policy was, in fact, incorporated into the faculty contract of employment, the court determined that the policy statement applied only to faculty members "who were dismissed." The court held that these faculty members, however, were not "dismissed"; instead, their contract terms merely expired and they were owed no further process than a notice of nonrenewal*.

The Contract of Employment
The contract of employment embodies the rights of the faculty member and his or her institution. These rights may be conferred formally by the actual words of the contract and informally by academic custom and usage, verbal assurances, and the unwritten practices of the institution.

The terms of the contract
Courts consider the contract of employment as containing

---

*The faculty members received their salaries through the end of their contracts.

the essential policies and practices of the institution as they relate to tenure, promotion, or contract renewals (Hendrickson 1991). Faculty employment contracts can range from simple letters of appointments to elaborate collective-bargaining agreements. The contract also may explicitly incorporate (or explicitly exclude) other institutional and professional policy statements, and courts may read these statements into the contract as evidence of academic practice (Kaplin 1985). These institutional and professional documents include the faculty handbook, other promotion and tenure policy statements, and the 1940 Statement of Principles. Occasionally, courts will look to the practices customarily engaged in by the institution to interpret the contract.

The terms of the contract, therefore, usually include the actual language in the notice of appointment, the faculty handbook or other institutional or professional documents, academic custom and practice, and in some cases, the oral and written assurances of certain key administrators. Institutions should ensure that these materials, customs, and promises are clear, unambiguous, and fairly consistent with each other.

The words of the contract

Courts first will look to the words of the contract (the letter of appointment) to determine the rights and obligations of the parties in resolving disputes about reappointment, promotion, or tenure. If the language is clear, unambiguous, and consistent, then courts will decide the case based upon the contract. Occasionally, some terms in the contract conflict. In *Halpin vs. LaSalle University* (1994), two faculty members sued the university claiming that their employment contract stipulated employment for the remainder of their lives, thus exempting them from the university's mandatory-retirement program. Their contract stated that the university was extending to each professor an "invitation to continue as a member of the faculty for the remainder of his academic life." But they received annual contracts. Later, the institution adopted a retirement program, calling for mandatory retirement at age 70. When the faculty members reached 70, they were notified that they had been retired. The court determined that the facts, taken as a whole, indicated that the professors were employed on term contracts.

In effect, the faculty members had a series of renewable one-year contracts and the age-70 retirement provision was incorporated into these contracts. This is a good example of a situation that could have been avoided if more care had been used in drafting the contract. Furthermore, as of Jan. 1, 1994, federal law has made mandatory-retirement programs illegal (see Section Four).

Academic custom and usage

When the language in the contract is ambiguous or there are gaps in the contract, courts will look to academic usage and custom to determine the rights and obligations of the institution and the faculty member. This custom and usage is embodied in institutional documents and practices and external policy statements (such as the 1940 Statement of Principles). In *Greene vs. Howard University* (1969), five untenured faculty members had been dismissed after an internal investigation indicated they had been involved in a number of disruptive incidents on campus. The university terminated their appointments as of the end of the academic year. The faculty members claimed they had a contractual right to adequate notice and a hearing before their appointments were terminated. The court agreed with the faculty members, holding that the practices customarily followed required the university to provide the faculty members with an opportunity to be heard. To determine what the university's customary practices were, the court looked to the faculty handbook, which was not specifically referenced in the contracts, and on the assurances of administrators about the common practices of the university in these types of situations.

To avoid such lawsuits, institutions should explicitly state in writing the terms and conditions for reappointment, promotion, or tenure. In *Marwil vs. Baker* (1980), a faculty member at the University of Michigan was informed in 1978 (his sixth year) that the next year would be his terminal year. He sued, alleging that it was the university's custom to give him a tenure review in his sixth year. The court held that under the university's then-current policy, implemented in 1974, he had no right to a tenure review. Under previous custom, however, he would have been entitled to a tenure review in his sixth year.

Since courts will look to internal and external documents

When the language in the contract is ambiguous or there are gaps in the contract, courts will look to academic usage and custom to determine the rights and obligations of the institution and the faculty member.

for guidance in resolving reappointment, promotion, or tenure disputes, administrators and faculty members should exercise care when drafting these materials; if there is any ambiguous language, it should be clarified. The contract also should be explicit about which institutional policies and practices are part of the employment contract.

Verbal assurances (oral or written)

In reviewing contracts of employment, courts examine the expressed words of the contracts. Courts also have looked to other materials as evidence of a contract, including oral or written assurances by key administrators. This is particularly troublesome for institutions, since many faculty members probably can remember a comment or statement made to them implying job security, promotion, or other issues (Hustoles 1983). Because these assurances are difficult to prove, courts are reluctant to consider verbal assurances or promises as granting any rights not explicitly stated in a contract. In *Beckwith vs. Rhode Island School of Design* (1979), a faculty member of graphic design claimed he had been promised a three-year contract by his department chairperson after completing a one-year trial period as an adjunct professor. The court determined that the promise had been made but held against the faculty member because the chairperson did not have the authority to bind the institution to such a contract (Hustoles 1983).

In *Soni vs. Board of Trustees of the University of Tennessee* (1975), however, a court held that verbal assurances were a part of the employment contract. Soni, a mathematics professor, claimed he was denied due process (see Section Three for a discussion of due process) when the university failed to renew his contract without giving him adequate notice or a hearing. Soni had been promised by the former and new department heads that he would be considered for a permanent position, but during a faculty meeting to discuss this issue it was pointed out that university regulations prevented the permanent appointments of persons who are not U.S. citizens. Soni was not a citizen. He was informed by the new head in 1968 that he would be appointed to associate professor but the issue of tenure would need to wait until he became a U.S. citizen. Soni also was included in the university's pension plan. The current head also assured Soni that he was "wanted" at the university and that his "prospects" were "good." Soni purchased a home in the area and stopped looking for employment elsewhere.

In 1972, Soni was informed that his appointment would be discontinued at the end of the academic year because his performance had not been of the "quality" expected of those to be granted tenure. In ruling that Soni legitimately relied upon the written and oral assurances, the court was persuaded that the verbal promises and assurances gave Soni a "reasonable expectation" of future and continued employment, entitling him to a due process hearing.

Soni illustrates that verbal assurances by the dean, department head, or other key administrator may create contractual rights and obligations; therefore, institutions should explicitly indicate which official or administrator has the authority to bind the institution to an employment contract (Hustoles 1983; see also *Beckwith vs. Rhode Island School of Design* 1979). This defense, however, is not always accepted by courts. In *Lewis vs. Loyola University of Chicago* (1986), oral promises and letters given by the dean to Lewis, a professor of medicine and chair of the pathology department at the university's medical school, assured Lewis during recruitment that he would be recommended for tenure within two years. The dean forgot to submit Lewis' candidacy. Just before his third year, Lewis received notice that the following year would be his final. The court found that the oral and written promises of the dean were a part of the employment contract and bound the institution, though the formal employment offer did not contain such promises.

Amending the contract

The contract of employment can be amended at any time as long as the institution and the faculty member agree. Contract rights also can be waived in writing by the parties or unintentionally by their actions (Kaplin and Lee 1995). In *Chung vs. Park* (1975), a faculty member at Mansfield College who was not reappointed after five years agreed to have the matter resolved by arbitration, which held against him. The faculty member then sued, alleging that the college did not follow its procedures. The court held that the faculty member and the institution had agreed to the arbitration and therefore were bound by it (Kaplin and Lee 1995). *Chung* notwithstanding, institutions and faculty members should ensure that any amendments to their contracts are in writing.

Oral assurances, however, generally will not amend the terms of an employment contract. In *Baker vs. Lafayette College* (1986), an assistant professor under a two-year contract claimed that the college breached his contract when he was not reappointed after his final year. Baker claimed that he was given oral assurances by the department head that he could expect more than two years of employment. The court held that oral terms cannot vary the terms of a written contract, and so he was not entitled to a contract renewal. Had the assurances been written, Baker might have prevailed.

Promotion and tenure criteria and procedures

Institutions have a great deal of discretion to decide how and when faculty members have satisfied the requirements for reappointment, promotion, or tenure. Courts usually will not interfere with an institution's substantive determination that a faculty member did not meet appropriate standards. Nor will courts interfere with the institution's discretion to establish what criteria will be used. For example, in *Levi vs. University of Texas at San Antonio* (1988), a faculty member was denied tenure for, among other reasons, a lenient grading policy. The court held that this criterion was reasonable given the university's mission.

Courts are more likely to review the procedures than the substance of such decisions. But institutions also have wide discretion in how they implement their procedures. In *Olson vs. Idaho State University* (1994), a faculty member had been an electronics instructor for five one-year terms. In his fifth year, he was recommended for tenure by his department tenure committee, the chairperson, and the dean. While the president was reviewing Olson's application, Olson was reprimanded by the dean for insubordination after initiating an unauthorized evaluation of another employee in violation of university policy. The dean also informed Olson that his application would be reviewed again. Subsequently, the president denied him tenure.

Olson claimed that he had done all that was required for tenure and that he was entitled to tenure because he was recommended by everyone except the president. The court held that according to the faculty handbook, tenure can only be conferred by the board of trustees. Since the president rejected his application before the board considered the matter, Olson had no legitimate claim to tenure. Olson also had claimed that contrary to the university's policies, the dean violated his contractual rights by revisiting his application. The court found no evidence that the dean actually revisited Olson's application.

In *Romer vs. Hobart and William Smith Colleges* (1994), a court also refused to interfere in an institution's decision to deny tenure, even when it may have violated its own procedures. In this case, a former classics professor alleged that his denial of tenure was based on an improper review process. His department recommended tenure, but the colleges' promotion and tenure committee recommended against tenure. The president agreed with the committee. Romer claimed that the promotion and tenure committee was influenced by information it received regarding a negative relationship he had with a colleague and that the committee's consideration of this information violated the procedures contained in the faculty handbook. The court held that even if the institution deviated from its procedures, its right to decide who shall receive tenure was not limited. Any limitation on the institution's discretion, the court indicated, must be expressly and explicitly stated in the contract.

Despite the rulings in *Olson* and *Romer*, institutions should follow their stated procedures. These procedures should be uniform for all faculty members (Centra 1993). Courts sometimes will rule in favor of faculty members when institutions fail to abide by their standard procedures. In *Ganguli vs. University of Minnesota* (1994), for example, the court held that a denial of tenure was arbitrary and capricious.

Ganguli was a faculty member of mathematics at the university. While she was preparing for her tenure review, the head of the department, who was charged with preparing her case for the tenure process, was removed from her case because of a perception by the department faculty that his behavior toward Ganguli was negative and judgmental. The dean appointed the head of another department to prepare her case for tenure review (usually members of the same department were so appointed). The university also solicited more than 40 external reviewers in Ganguli's case (the norm was six to 10), which mostly were positive. A majority of the department and college faculties voted in favor of tenure and promotion, and the promotion and tenure committee voted

3-to-1 in Ganguli's favor, with one abstention. The head of her case recommended tenure to the dean, but his letter criticized her research and publication record, despite the department faculty's criticism of his analysis of Ganguli's case.

The dean recommended promotion and tenure to the provost but noted that her case was "not the strongest." The provost believed that the no-votes and the abstention indicated that Ganguli did not have a "compelling" case for tenure, and he rejected her application. The university's promotion and tenure regulations did not require a "compelling" case, and they prohibited the consideration of abstentions as negative votes. It was clear to the court that the university did not abide by its own standards of procedure in reviewing Ganguli's application for tenure, especially in choosing someone from outside of her department to prepare her case, soliciting so many external reviewers, requiring a "compelling" case for tenure, and counting an abstention as a negative vote. The court mandated a new review. This case illustrates the importance of adhering to written policies.

The Employment Contract and State Law

Although tenure rights are primarily created by contract, state law also may create rights and obligations for public institutions. In some cases, the state's law supersedes institutional authority. In *Faculty of the City University of New York Law School at Queens College vs. Murphy* (1989), the chancellor refused to forward to the board of trustees the tenure applications of two law-school faculty members who failed to receive unanimous support from the tenure committee. The court held that state law established the board of trustees as having exclusive authority to grant tenure and therefore the chancellor did not have the authority to withhold the applications.

Tenure rights may be created or revoked by state law. If they are revoked, the institution may choose to ignore them unless they have been promised in an employment contract. Contractual rights, however, may not be revoked by state law unless a contract explicitly provided for such a change (Kaplin and Lee 1995).

Part-Time Faculty Members and Adjunct Professors

The number of part-time faculty members and adjuncts is

increasing in higher education for a number of reasons but mainly because the employment of these faculty members is considerably cheaper than that of full-time, tenure-track faculty members (Gappa 1984; Kaplin and Lee 1995). These faculty members have specific needs (see Gappa 1984; Gappa and Leslie 1993). Institutions should pay particular attention to how these faculty members are experiencing their work environments. Often, they are not entitled to tenure, promotion, or other benefits, so their legal standing may be tenuous.

Although we will not directly discuss particular legal issues involving part-time faculty members and adjunct professors, a few words about them are important. The primary basis for the rights of part-time faculty members and adjunct professors is the employment contract, although state law may govern in this area as well (Kaplin and Lee 1995). Any rights extended to part-time faculty members should be specified in the contract. The 1940 Statement of Principles applies to full-time faculty members, not to adjuncts and part-time faculty. But institutions may choose to grant part-time faculty members the same rights. The advantages and disadvantages of extending further rights to these faculty members is beyond the scope of this report. If these faculty members are to be treated differently, then administrators should clearly understand the legal distinctions between both sets of faculty members and they should consult with the institution's attorney to ensure that the institution's policies express any desired difference between the two sets of faculty.

Tenure by Default
Courts recognize four methods of acquiring tenure (McKee 1980). *Automatic tenure* occurs when a faculty member attains tenure by being reemployed after a specified period. An example of this might be a policy that states that faculty members shall have tenure after three years of acceptable service. *Tenure by grant* is discretionary and requires some official institutional act or recognition that the faculty member has tenure (approval by the board of trustees, for example). De facto tenure is conferred by some reference to institutional rules or practices, or the understanding of the parties. This method of acquiring tenure may occur when a faculty member is given extensive assurances that he or she

had tenure, despite the existence of policies requiring some official act. And *tenure by default* occurs when a faculty member fulfills all of the eligibility requirements and is employed beyond the probationary period (McKee 1980). Automatic tenure and tenure by grant are explicitly established by the institution, while de facto tenure and tenure by default are judicially determined (McKee 1980). The discussion in the previous sections primarily related to the rights and obligations regarding automatic tenure and tenure by grant. De facto tenure is based upon the constitutional principles established by the Supreme Court in *Perry vs. Sindermann* (1972) and will be discussed further in the next section.

Tenure by default is based upon principles of contract law. If an institution is silent as to the method of acquiring tenure, its faculty members may attain tenure by default. And if the custom or practice at an institution indicates otherwise, faculty members may attain tenure by default despite specific language stating that tenure must be officially granted by the president or the governing board.

Since tenure by default is based upon the employment contract, the contract should be drafted carefully, and the institution that does not wish to confer tenure in such a manner will need to carefully adhere to its written standards and procedures. Since the employment contract may incorporate other institutional documents and policy statements, these materials also should be carefully reviewed. McKee pointed out that this is where institutions get into legal trouble, for although the employment contracts may be drafted with care, institutional tenure policies may not be. These policies usually are written collegially and reflect negotiation and compromise; as a result, they may not be legally tight, thereby leaving room for judicial interpretation.

Institutional practices also are important. Courts will use academic custom and usage to help interpret a contract that is silent or ambiguous about how tenure is acquired. Tenure by default is premised on the notion that a faculty member who is employed beyond the probationary period received tenure because he or she wasn't discontinued earlier. If the employment contract is silent or ambiguous about what constitutes a probationary period, courts may interpret the probationary period to be that established by the 1940 Statement of Principles, or seven years.

In *Bruno vs. Detroit Institute of Technology* (1974), the court held that reappointing a faculty member beyond the probationary period may confer tenure, even if the institution's policies specifically indicate that tenure can only be conferred by some affirmative act. Bruno had been reappointed from 1959 through 1966, when he was discontinued. The institution's tenure policy indicated that a faculty member who, in the opinion of the president and deans, has "acceptably performed" his or her duties for a period of three consecutive years, "has been assigned the rank of Associate or Full Professor, and has been tendered his fourth or succeeding annual contract and has accepted same, shall be considered to hold tenure" (p. 747). The institution claimed that the term "shall be considered to hold tenure" required an affirmative grant of tenure, and that administrators had not determined that Bruno had "acceptably performed" his duties. The court rejected both arguments, holding that the reappointment of Bruno beyond the probationary period provided the necessary "affirmative act" and the fact that he was continually reappointed indicated that the institution believed him to be performing acceptably.

The Supreme Court also indicated in *Perry vs. Sindermann* (1972) that institutional practice may provide a basis for conferring tenure. Institutions are vulnerable to judicial awards of tenure when their contracts are silent as to how tenure is to be attained or where the actions of the administrators indicate that tenure was conferred to a particular faculty member. For example, in *Soni vs. Board of Trustees of the University of Tennessee* (1975), discussed previously, the court held that promises made by the department head and letters sent to the faculty member gave him a reasonable expectation that he would be tenured, even though he had not been formally granted tenure as required by institutional policy.

If the institution does not wish to confer tenure in this manner, its employment contracts and other policy statements should clearly indicate that employment beyond the probationary period does not automatically confer tenure. The institution that seeks to modify its policies should be careful, however, to recognize that faculty members hired under earlier rules may have to be reviewed under policies in effect when they were hired. In *Honore vs. Douglas* (1987), a faculty member at the Thurgood Marshall School of

Law of Texas Southern University served for four years before being granted three consecutive one-year leaves of absence to serve in the Peace Corps. When he returned, the university refused to grant him tenure and released him three years later. When Honore first was hired, the university automatically conferred tenure after seven years of service. This policy was changed while he was away; tenure had to be officially conferred by the board of regents. When Honore was informed by the dean that he would not be rehired at the end of the year, he claimed he had automatic tenure under the old rules, and he sought confirmation of this from the Rank and Tenure Committee (which unanimously recommended tenure). He was denied tenure by the university and he sued, alleging a violation of due process rights. The trial court dismissed Honore's claims without allowing him to prove his case to a jury. The appeals court determined that since Honore was hired under an automatic-tenure policy, taught for four years, was on authorized leave for three years, and returned to work during his eighth year, a jury could determine that he had a legitimate claim to tenure.

Courts' willingness to confer tenure by default is relatively rare. Most courts still defer to institutional decisions. In *Hill vs. Talledega College* (1987), discussed previously, one of the faculty members alleged that he was entitled to tenure because he had been employed for 10 years at the college, and according to the 1940 Statement of Principles he should have tenure. The court noted that the 1940 Statement of Principles does not require the granting of tenure after seven years, but only states that tenure should be granted. Also, the court determined that the faculty handbook clearly indicated that tenure is granted by the board of trustees and that the acquisition of tenure is not automatic after seven years. The existence of conflicting policy statements in this and other cases led to lawsuits that could have been avoided had institutions ensured their policies were consistent.

"Tenure Density"

The financial cost of tenure and other policy considerations have caused some institutions to place quotas on the number of faculty who may be tenured in a given department or college (see Mortimer, Bagshaw, and Masland 1985). When the number of tenured faculty reaches the maximum allowed percentage, then "tenure density" has occurred. Courts generally will defer to institutions to determine what criteria is to be used in tenure decisions, and this includes tenure density.

In *Coe vs. Board of Regents of the University of Wisconsin* (1987), a female faculty member in the sociology department at the University of Wisconsin-Stevens Point was recommended for tenure by the department tenure committee, even though the department was "over-tenured." Institutional policy capped the number of tenured professors at 80 percent of the total faculty in a given department. As a result, the chancellor denied her tenure. Coe contended that because tenure density is not an enumerated criterion under Wisconsin law, the chancellor exceeded his authority in considering it. Wisconsin law provided that tenure shall be made in "accordance with the mission and needs of the particular institution and its component parts." The faculty senate had approved the tenure policy, establishing tenure density as a criterion in determining whether a faculty member can be tenured. The court upheld the university's decision not to grant Coe tenure because state law authorized the institution to make tenure decisions in light of its needs, and the faculty determined that capping the number of tenured faculty served those needs.

Courts generally will defer to institutions to determine what criteria is to be used in tenure decisions, and this includes tenure density.

Another court upheld a tenure-density policy in *Sola vs. Lafayette College* (1986). In this case, the college had a policy capping the number of tenured faculty in a given department at two-thirds of the total faculty, unless there was an "exceptional 'guideline-breaking'" candidate. Sola, an assistant professor of psychology, was denied tenure by the tenure committee (the vote was tied, resulting in a denial under the college's rules). The department chairman had recommended tenure to the committee, but he noted that a stronger, male faculty member was coming up for tenure and Sola's application should not jeopardize this professor's candidacy. Sola's appeal to the president was denied and she sued the college alleging, among other issues, that the tenure quota violated the academic freedom of the faculty members to decide tenure issues. The court held that the college may use a tenure quota as a criterion for determining who should be tenured, and that academic freedom would be more threatened by the court's interference in these internal matters.

On an interesting note, Sola was permitted to raise the issue that language in the faculty handbook permitting affirmative action to be considered in employment decisions could be construed as a contractual obligation. Specifically, Sola argued that since the college did not consider her gender as a positive factor, it breached the employment contract. The court determined that Sola could present this to the jury as a legitimate breach of contract claim. Affirmative action will be discussed in more depth in Section Five, but it is important to note here that colleges or universities may be required to abide by language in institutional policy statements promoting or authorizing the affirmative action.

Faculty members may be legally denied tenure because an institution or the department is "over-tenured," and so institutions may develop these policies to deal with financial constraints. For example, three faculty members recently were denied tenure by the board of trustees of the University of Massachusetts System because 79 percent of the faculty already had tenure (*Chronicle of Higher Education*, Sept. 8, 1995). It appears that the only legal basis for challenging these decisions is the employment contract if it precludes using tenure density as a criterion for granting tenure. Faculty members, however, are unlikely to succeed in challenges to tenure-density policies. Court deference to institutions in employment matters is very strong. If institutions wish to establish tenure density as criterion in reappointment, promotion, or tenure decisions and this is clear or not precluded in the contract of employment, courts will not interfere.

Financial Exigency and Program Elimination or Reduction

Some institutions, faced with heavy budget reductions, may be required to eliminate or reduce some faculty positions or programs. Courts give great deference to an institution's . claims about its financial situation and its decisions during a financial crisis (Johnson 1981; Olswang 1992). Institutions, therefore, should always reserve the right to eliminate faculty and programs because of financial exigency.

Faculty members negatively affected by these financial decisions may sue the institution under a number of legal claims, including denial of due process and breach of contract (Johnson 1981). The institution, however, may eliminate tenured or untenured positions when it is in financial difficulty, as long as the criteria are clear and not arbitrarily applied (Olswang 1982). Tenured faculty members at public institutions are entitled to due process before their positions are eliminated, although tenure provides little protection when an institution is under serious financial difficulty. Many institutions adhere to AAUP guidelines regarding staff reductions, which permit elimination of tenured positions, although they require a finding of "bona fide" financial exigency (AAUP 1990). Courts have looked to AAUP guidelines when dealing with the elimination of tenured positions for financial exigency (*AAUP vs. Bloomfield College* 1974).

Untenured faculty members, however, have little protection from contract nonrenewals. Courts will look to the employment contract and other institutional policies and practices to determine the rights and obligations of the parties in these situations. In *Knowles vs. Unity College* (1981), the college canceled its tenure policy in 1971 due to financial problems. Knowles, who had not achieved tenure before the policy was repealed, was not reappointed and was given no formal statement of the reasons. Knowles sued, claiming that since the college had adopted AAUP guidelines, he was entitled to tenure (he had been employed from 1969 to 1978). The court held that since the college did not have a tenure policy, he was not entitled to tenure. The court noted, however, that the official statements by the administration, and the AAUP guidelines, may have given Knowles an implied contract, entitling him to a contract renewal. If the contract guarantees particular notice requirements, courts will enforce these provisions. In *Zimmerman vs. Minor College* (1972), the court enforced a contract provision giving faculty members who had served for more than two years at least 12 months' notice before being dismissed and held the institution liable for the faculty member's annual salary.

The AAUP Standards for Notice of Nonreappointment requires 12 months' notice in advance of dismissal for a faculty member employed for more than two years (AAUP 1990). This requirement is sound practice because it provides faculty members with an opportunity to challenge claims of financial exigency and gives a faculty member opportunity to seek other employment. Furthermore, if the contract is silent, courts may use the AAUP guidelines as evidence of academic practice.

Courts are reluctant to question an institution's decisions during a financial crisis. Administrators usually are permitted to make these decisions without faculty approval, even if faculty approval was sought in other matters. In *Ahmadieh et al. vs. State Board of Agriculture* (1988), for example, tenured faculty members, whose positions were eliminated as a result of a reorganization of academic programs at the University of Southern Colorado, alleged that the governing board's decision failed to follow certain handbook procedures. Specifically, the faculty members alleged that all recommended program changes had to be approved by the faculty senate. The court construed the language as only applying to faculty-generated proposals. And the court held that the board's authority over curriculum and program development was limited only by state law, and the faculty senate could not be vested with such authority under state law.

In contract matters, the institution has a great deal of discretion in determining its reappointment, promotion, or tenure criteria. The institution may base its decisions upon tenure quotas or the financial situation of the institution. Institutions, however, should explicitly and unambiguously state how tenure is to be conferred, what criteria will be used, and under what situations faculty members will be dismissed. Furthermore, institutions should give faculty members adequate notice of nonrenewal, and the notice should indicate that the reason for nonreappointment is financial exigency. This protects the faculty members' reputation, and in public institutions the threat to a faculty member's reputation implicates "liberty interests*," necessitating due process protection (Johnson 1981, p. 302).

Collective Bargaining

Collective-bargaining agreements (that is, faculty union contracts) are common sources of contractual rights and obligations for faculty members and institutions, but they present some of the most complex legal issues. Collective bargaining is one of the few areas in which institutions must deal with

---

*"Liberty interests" are discussed more extensively in Section Three.

"outsiders", for example, labor-relations boards, arbitrators, and, of course, the courts (Kaplin and Lee 1995). Collective-bargaining issues also force institutions to grapple with major policy issues: To what extent do collective-bargaining agreements force conflicts between administrative license and faculty self-governance? Can traditional collective-bargaining subjects such as seniority be reconciled with tenure and merit? And how does the participation of the "outsiders" affect institutional autonomy? (Kaplin 1985).

Collective bargaining is important for several reasons. Most significantly, if the faculty at a particular institution is unionized, then the institution may have to negotiate with it for reappointment, promotion, or tenure policies and procedures. In some states, almost all faculty members at public institutions are unionized, and many faculty in private institutions also bargain collectively with their institutions. Because there is more strength in numbers, collective bargaining gives the faculty more power to negotiate with their institutions about employment matters. Furthermore, at private institutions, faculty members are allowed to strike if they are unable to agree on some aspects of their contract. Faculty at public institutions usually are prohibited from striking, but there are other remedies available to them.

Administrators also may find collective bargaining advantageous. Collective bargaining allows the faculty to negotiate with the institution as one voice, rather than many. Furthermore, problems may be channeled into a grievance and arbitration procedure (as is often called for in these types of contracts). The use of binding arbitration often is cheaper than litigation.

Private collective bargaining is governed by federal legislation: the National Labor Relations Act of 1935 (NLRA) as subsequently amended. The National Labor Relations Board, or NLRB, has jurisdiction over the certification of unions and complaints of unfair labor practices, and it makes its decisions on a case-by-case basis. The NLRB extended its jurisdiction to faculty members in 1971 in *C.W. Post Center of Long Island University* (Kaplin and Lee 1995).

Public collective bargaining is governed by state law, not by the federal NLRA. Thirty-five states permit at least some forms of collective bargaining in higher education. Often, state law covers public employees in general and makes little distinction for faculty members (Kaplin and Lee 1995).

It is difficult to generalize about public collective bargaining because the law varies between states, and there are few administrative or judicial precedents. Many state labor-relations boards and courts, however, are guided by the federal law principles and thus the issues discussed in this report also may apply to public institutions.

Religious institutions and collective bargaining

The issue of whether religious institutions are subject to NLRB jurisdiction is unsettled and as a result will not be further addressed in this report. The Supreme Court ruled in *NLRB vs. Catholic Bishop of Chicago* (1979) that Congress did not intend for the NLRB to have jurisdiction over teachers in a church-related school. This case, however, did not involve higher education. The very few cases that have involved NLRB jurisdiction over religious institutions have not resolved this issue.

The collective-bargaining agreement

When faculty members decide they want to bargain collectively, representatives can request that the institution bargain with the faculty as a group (that is, with the union). An institution should wait until the union is certified by the NLRB or state labor-relations board before bargaining with it because it is illegal to exclusively bargain with a union that is not supported by a majority of the faculty (Kaplin and Lee 1995). Once the union is certified as the bargaining agent of the faculty, it is the exclusive bargaining agent for the faculty no matter if other faculty members become union members, are not willing to be represented, or agree with the terms of the collective-bargaining agreement. In *Neiman vs. Kingsborough Community College* (1989), a faculty member filed a breach-of-contract claim when he was not reappointed by the college. The collective-bargaining agreement called for a three-step grievance process, but the faculty member refused to request binding arbitration, the third step of the process. The court dismissed the faculty member's lawsuit, holding that his sole remedy lay in the grievance procedures called for by the collective-bargaining agreement.

The institution and the union may negotiate on any subject, although some subjects are considered "mandatory," some "permissible," and others "prohibited." A mandatory subject must be negotiated (salaries, for example). A permissible subject is one for which the parties may, but are not required to, negotiate (faculty lounges, for example). Both parties must agree to negotiate over permissible subjects. A prohibited subject, of course, such as a fire-alarm system, may not be negotiated.

Mandatory subjects must be negotiated and include wages, hours, and other terms and conditions of employment. Failure to bargain in good faith (honestly and fairly) about mandatory subjects is considered an unfair labor practice (Kaplin and Lee 1995). The question of whether the terms for reappointment, promotion, or tenure are considered mandatory is difficult to answer. Some courts have held that rules governing tenure (such as the criteria and way the criteria are measured) are not mandatory subjects for negotiation. For example, a New Jersey court held in *Association of New Jersey State College Faculties vs. Dungan* (1974) that the authority to determine the tenure criteria had been delegated to the board of education by state law, and thus tenure criteria were not negotiable. Other courts have determined that tenure rules are negotiable.

In *Hackel vs. Vermont State Colleges* (1981), for example, a Vermont court held that promotion and tenure issues are negotiable under its state labor laws. Five faculty members had been granted tenure by their college presidents, but the chancellor of the Vermont State Colleges asked the board of trustees to override the college presidents' actions. The board claimed that promotion and tenure could not be negotiated and that it had authority over those matters. The court determined that the collective-bargaining agreement gave college presidents the power to make final determinations in promotion and tenure cases.

Even in states in which tenure rules are not negotiable, the faculty may be able to negotiate with their institutions for the *process* to be used in making such decisions. In *Snitow vs. Rutgers University* (1986), a New Jersey court held that although the criteria for determining tenure are not negotiable, the process to be followed is. A faculty member had been denied tenure and filed a grievance. The grievance committee determined that the tenure committee acted arbitrarily by permitting a person known to be biased against the faculty member's research to vote on her application. Under the collective-bargaining agreement she had to exhaust all her administrative remedies before suing, but the faculty member filed the lawsuit before the review process was completed. The court held that the grievance process was properly negotiated and dismissed her case because she did not exhaust her administrative remedies before filing litigation.

Eligibility of full-time faculty members for collective bargaining

The NLRA and many state labor laws exclude "supervisors" from their coverage, and courts have created a "managerial" exclusion. The cases involving faculty members have focused on the "managers" exclusion, not "supervisors." The major issue for many institutions, therefore, is whether their faculty members are "managers," thereby making them ineligible to bargain as employees. Institutions *may* bargain with faculty members considered "managers"; but they are *not required to* under federal or state labor law, and any agreement so negotiated is not enforceable in court by the institution or the union.

What are "managers"? Managers are those employees who are involved in developing and enforcing the employer's policies. The rationale for excluding supervisors from NLRA protection is that employers should be able to expect loyalty from them. The judicially created exclusion of managers is rationalized on the notion that managers have access to businesses' confidential information. Courts have not focused on whether faculty members *should* be considered managers but *whether they are*. And courts have made these determinations on a case-by-case basis. The Supreme Court, in *NLRB vs. Yeshiva University* (1980), addressed this issue, probably causing more confusion and litigation and creating much controversy in academia.

NLRB vs. Yeshiva University (1980)

In 1975, the faculty at Yeshiva University attempted to form a union and sought certification from the NLRB. The university opposed the petition on the grounds that the faculty members were managerial or supervisory and therefore exempt from NLRA coverage. The NLRB certified the union. The university refused to bargain with the union, claiming that the faculty members were heavily involved in institutional governance and so it was not required to recognize the union. When the union filed an unfair labor practice complaint against the university, the NLRB sued in federal court to seek enforcement of its decision. The Supreme Court, by a mere 5-4 majority indicating the great disagreement within the court, held that Yeshiva's full-time faculty members were "managerial" and excluded from NLRA protection.

The court defined managerial employees as those who develop and enforce employer policies. The Yeshiva faculty, the Supreme Court determined, were "unquestionably" managerial because they exercised authority over academic matters (the offering and scheduling of courses, teaching of courses, grading policies, and admission and graduation standards, for example), administrative matters (they made recommendations regarding the size of the university, the tuition charged, and the location of the school), and faculty employment matters (they made recommendations in all hiring, tenure, sabbaticals, dismissals, and promotion cases). The court noted that although the administration had the final decision in these matters, the overwhelming majority of recommendations were implemented.

The Supreme Court was not willing to hold that faculty members at all institutions were managerial. The court indicated which institutions' faculty were permitted to bargain collectively:

> It is plain, for example, that professors may not be excluded merely because they determine the content of their own courses, evaluate their own students, and supervise their own research. There thus may be institutions of higher learning unlike Yeshiva where the faculty are entirely or predominantly non-managerial. There may also be faculty members at Yeshiva and like universities who properly could be included in a bargaining unit. It may be that a rational line could be drawn between tenured and untenured faculty members, depending on how a faculty is structured and operates (pp. 866-7).

There were four dissenters in the case who disagreed with the majority that these (or perhaps all) faculty members were managerial. Justice William Brennan, writing for the dissenters, claimed that the administration retained the ultimate decision-making authority at the university, not the faculty. Furthermore, he contended, the board has always construed managerial to mean those employees who are "true representatives of management." Faculty members, on the other hand, influence decision-making solely because of their collective expertise, not because they are managers or supervisors. They are not accountable to the administration nor are their interests necessarily aligned. Brennan claimed that to say that a faculty member's professional competence could depend on his or her loyalty to the administration is "antithetical" to the concept of academic freedom.

The managerial exclusion, apparently, applies only to those faculty at "Yeshiva-like" or "mature*" universities. This case seems to indicate that faculty members at research institutions may not be covered under the NLRA. But even at those institutions, it is unlikely that all faculty can be excluded from collective bargaining; part-time faculty members, instructors, lecturers, visiting professors, and untenured professors may be considered sufficiently nonmanagerial and able to bargain collectively (Kaplin and Lee 1995).

Yeshiva and Public Collective Bargaining
While *Yeshiva* attempts to determine who may bargain collectively in private higher education, it also impacts collective bargaining in the public sector. In addition to potentially deterring faculty members at public institutions from assuming more active roles in institutional governance, the *Yeshiva* decision is likely to affect how states develop collective-bargaining laws; and because state labor laws are similar to the NLRA, state courts and labor-relations boards may use the decision to guide their interpretation of these laws (Nagle 1994).

In *University of Pittsburgh* (1990), a faculty union sought to bargain collectively with the university, claiming that the faculty were not managerial, and Pennsylvania's law should not be interpreted to consider them managers. The university claimed that the faculty were managerial under the *Yeshiva* definition, and the state law should be interpreted consistently with *Yeshiva*. The faculty and the university had agreed that the governance structure was similar to that of Yeshiva University, and so the issue in this case was whether

---

*The Supreme Court used this term but did not define it. Presumably, it applied to large research institutions in which faculty have autonomy in many areas.

the faculty at the University of Pittsburgh could bargain collectively. The hearing officer for the Pennsylvania Labor Relations Board held that the *Yeshiva* analysis was appropriate for determining the status of faculty at Pennsylvania institutions. Stressing the faculty members' participation in university governance, the hearing officer determined that the full-time faculty at the University of Pittsburgh were managerial (see Nagle 1994).

The hearing officer's ruling was reversed by the full board, which ruled that the faculty may unionize. But ironically, the faculty voted to reject union representation (Kaplin and Lee 1995). The *Yeshiva* decision applies to collective bargaining at private institutions, an area covered by federal law (that is, the NLRA). Public collective bargaining is governed by state law. The application of *Yeshiva* to collective bargaining at public institutions has not been completely successful. Some states permit its public employees, including faculty members, to unionize. But the *Yeshiva* decision has had an impact on public labor law. A few states amended their labor laws to more align them with the *Yeshiva* holding (see Nagel 1994). And as we saw in the hearing officer's ruling in *University of Pittsburgh* (1990), state courts and labor-relations boards may interpret their laws as restricting the unionization of faculty members considered managerial.

Are faculty members at private institutions eligible for collective bargaining?

The answer to this question depends on whether the faculty members are so sufficiently involved in institutional governance so as to be termed managers. Full-time faculty members at large research institutions are probably managers, but this may not be necessarily so. The NLRB makes rulings on whether faculty members are eligible for collective bargaining on a case-by-case basis, which makes it difficult to generalize to all institutions. The case law, however, does provide some (but not much) assistance to administrators. At institutions in which the faculty has no input into policy decisions, key administrators make most of the important decisions, and the faculty's recommendations are not consistently accepted, the faculty is likely to be eligible to unionize (see *Bradford College* 1982; *NLRB vs. Florida Memorial College* 1987; *NLRB vs. Stephens Institute* 1980). In *Loretto*

Heights College vs. NLRB (1984), a court determined that since the faculty role in institutional governance occurs mainly through committees, they were not managerial. The court noted that in light of the infrequent nature of committee work, the mixed membership of the committees, and the layers of administrative approval required for many decisions, faculty participation in institutional governance fell "far short" of that contemplated by *Yeshiva.*

Faculties that have substantial decision-making authority are likely to be considered managerial and therefore not protected by federal or state law. Administrators in these cases may refuse to negotiate with their faculties' representatives. As we saw in *Yeshiva,* a faculty that essentially controls the curriculum, grading policies, course offerings and scheduling, admission and graduation standards, hiring, promotion, and tenure decisions and other important areas is likely to fall within the judicially created managerial exemption to the NLRA. In addition, if the administration accepts the overwhelming majority of faculty recommendations, the managerial exemption may apply (see *Duquesne University* 1982; *Ithaca College* 1982; *Thiel College* 1982). The NLRB, however, also has certified a faculty union, even when the administration accepts the majority of the faculty's recommendations (*Lewis University* 1982).

The NLRB's policy of not creating general standards for when faculty members can be considered managerial and thus unable to bargain collectively leaves administrators and faculty members with little guidance and few legal answers. The decisions appear contradictory, and the NLRB has not taken into consideration the nature of faculty governance; rather, the NLRB has chosen only to limit its analysis to the criteria established in *Yeshiva* (Lee and Begin 1983).

Certain conditions seem to influence NLRB decisions:

1. The degree to which faculty recommendations are accepted;
2. The role of key administrators (deans and department heads, for example) with regard to these recommendations; and
3. The language in the employment contract and other institutional policy statements purporting to reserve the institution's management to the administration or which gives faculty significant governance authority and the degree to

which the actual practice matches the words in these documents (Lee and Begin 1983).

Since these conditions are controlled by the administration, the issue of whether faculty members are managerial may depend on the make-up of the administration and its beliefs about faculty self-governance.

Apparently, the *Yeshiva* decision prevents unionization at large research institutions (or other "mature" institutions) in which faculty governance is firmly established and its control over reappointment, promotion, or tenure decisions is stable enough to survive changes in administrative personnel (Lee and Begin 1983). Faculty members and administrators at all institutions wishing to address collective-bargaining issues, however, should consult with experienced administrators, and most importantly, the expert advice of attorneys specializing in academic labor law.

XYZ College Scenarios

Let us return to the scenarios described at the beginning of the section. Clearly, if the college is experiencing financial difficulties tenure would not protect Professor A. If Professor A has tenure, he may be able to resume his position (because the college only eliminated untenured positions) or the college may have to prove that the financial difficulties warranting the dismissal of a tenured faculty member were bona fide. It appears, however, that Professor A's claim to tenure probably was not valid. The handbook stated that faculty members must prove merit in three areas before tenure is conferred and also that faculty members must apply for tenure in their sixth year. This language indicated that tenure is not to be conferred automatically after the completion of a seventh year of service.

The main question here is whether Professor A should have been eligible to apply for tenure. The answer depends on how "full time" is defined. The handbook stated that only full-time faculty members are eligible for tenure, and a strong argument exists that Professor A had not been a full-time faculty member for seven years. Courts likely will look to other documents and institutional custom to determine whether Professor A was "full time" for the necessary period of time. It is possible that Professor A may prove that the college generally considers some adjuncts as "full time" in

...the issue of whether faculty members are managerial may depend on the make-up of the administration and its beliefs about faculty self-governance.

similar situations. The assurances by the department chairperson also may be evidence of this custom as well. Ordinarily, however, courts will look to the plain meaning of the language in the employment contract, and this means that Professor A was not a full-time faculty member for the necessary period of time.

The issue of whether faculty members at XYZ College may form a union is very complicated. Much of it depends on whether they were managerial. The NLRB would consider the extent to which they are involved in institutional governance, how administrators deal with faculty input, and whether the administration overwhelmingly accepts the faculty's recommendations. It appears that the faculty had extensive authority over academic matters (as was the case in *Yeshiva*). Although it was not clear how often the administration overturns its recommendations in employment matters, the faculty had less autonomy in this area than in the academic area. Its participation in committees can be viewed in two ways: On one hand, the administration was involved in the governance of institution through committees and its input was often sought; on the other hand, its authority was diminished by committee participation, which may have had mixed membership and met infrequently. It was unclear how the college viewed these committees and whether its recommendations were significantly accepted. The NLRB and courts have dealt with faculty members' eligibility for collective bargaining on a case-by-case basis, making it difficult, at this point, to provide many general guiding principles in these matters.

Summary

The faculty contract of employment includes the letter of appointment and professional and institutional policies governing reappointment, promotion, or tenure decisions. These policies often include the faculty handbook and a number of AAUP policy statements, if referenced. But even if these documents are not explicitly incorporated into the contract of employment, courts may refer to them as evidence of academic practice, custom, and usage, especially when the contract is inconsistent or ambiguous. Administrators should recognize that the 1940 Statement of Principles is incorporated into the employment contract by many institutions, and courts commonly refer to it in resolving tenure disputes.

Administrators should consider reviewing their policy statements to ensure that they are explicit, unambiguous, and consistent, and that they illustrate the desired rights and obligations regarding reappointment, promotion, or tenure decisions. Careful attention also must be paid to those practices not specifically addressed in any written document. Occasionally, a particular practice (customarily providing a statement of reasons, even if not specifically called for in the contract, for example) may be incorporated as part of the employment contract. Furthermore, the promises and assurances of key administrators can bind the institution to a contractual obligation and so the institution should clearly indicate and communicate which administrators can bind the institution to an employment contract.

Collective-bargaining agreements may govern how faculty members are reappointed, promoted, or tenured. Federal labor law, which governs private collective bargaining, does not cover faculty members who are considered managers. Thus, the institution may refuse to bargain with its representatives. It appears that faculty members at large research institutions may be considered managers. Faculty members at public institutions are permitted to bargain solely based on authority granted under state law. Some states permit faculty members to unionize. Collective bargaining is an extremely complex and unsettled area of law, and institutions should seek expert legal and administrative assistance in dealing with such matters.

CONSTITUTIONAL RIGHTS IN EMPLOYMENT DECISIONS: DUE PROCESS, FREE SPEECH, AND ACADEMIC FREEDOM

Consider these scenarios:

You recently were notified that you were denied tenure at Eastern State University, a public research institution, and that your services no longer would be required as of the end of the next academic year. Your department narrowly voted in favor of tenure, but the dean, the vice president for academic affairs, and the president rejected your application. The faculty hand-book states clearly that the probation period is six years, at the end of which the faculty member will have tenure or be awarded a one-year terminal con-tract. The handbook also states tenure is not automat-ic and that "tenure can only be conferred by the board of trustees after a determination that the faculty mem-ber has proven merit in teaching, research, and ser-vice." The handbook adds further that the university abides by and supports the 1940 Statement of Principles. You have been employed at the university for seven years, but three of those years were as an instructor. Under university policy, instructors are not eligible for tenure. You believe that since you have been employed as a full-time teacher for longer than six years, you should have tenure under the universi-ty's policy.

You also believe you were denied tenure in retalia-tion for public criticisms you have made regarding the university's investment in South Africa and its treatment of women and people of color. The university claims that your teaching skills are "poor," and that you have very few publications.

How do you think a court would rule regarding your claim for tenure? Does the Constitution provide you with any protection? How would a court rule regarding your claim that you were denied tenure in retaliation for your criticisms of Eastern State University?

This section addresses the rights and responsibilities of faculty members and institutions under the Constitution. Faculty members at public institutions have been able to claim numerous rights under the Constitution. This section focuses on rights established by the First and 14th amend-ments, specifically the rights of due process, free speech, and academic freedom as they relate to reappointment, promotion, and tenure decisions. This discussion focuses solely on public institutions, since private institutions are not subject to these particular constitutional protections. Nevertheless, administrators at private colleges and universities should be aware that if they guarantee due process or freedom-of-speech rights in their contracts, courts will require that these institutions provide their faculty members the same protection expected by the Constitution. In other words, courts will define due process and free speech just as they would for constitutional reasons.

Due Process rights arise from the 14th Amendment and apply to faculty members who have "property" or "liberty" interests. The Constitution does not guarantee any property or liberty interests; it only protects their being abridged "without due process." Essentially, the 14th Amendment prohibits the institution from depriving or denying a faculty member his or her "property" and "liberty" interests without first providing him or her with certain procedural safeguards. This section will address the legal parameters of "property" and "liberty" interests.

Institutions also are prohibited from denying reappointment, promotion, or tenure to a faculty member because of that faculty member's exercise of his or her freedom of speech or exercise of academic freedom. The second half of this section will focus on what constitutes freedom of speech and academic freedom and the institution and faculty member's rights and responsibilities regarding these interests.

Due Process Rights

Under the 14th Amendment no state shall "deprive any person of life, *liberty*, or *property*, without *due process* of law." Faculty members at public institutions are entitled to *due process* if they have a property or liberty interest in their employment. Courts have considered tenured faculty members as having a "property interest" in their employment and so they are entitled to certain due process rights before they can be dismissed. Untenured faculty members do not have a legitimate expectation of continued employment — unlike tenured faculty members — beyond the terms of their contracts. In fact, they are not legally entitled to be informed of the reasons for nonreappointment, although many institutions provide such information. These faculty members, on the other hand, have a "property interest" in their employment while their contracts are in effect. For the duration of their term contracts, they have legally enforceable agreements. Untenured faculty members also may sometimes hold de facto tenure, which entitles them to the protection afforded by the due process clause of the 14th Amendment.

Untenured faculty members also are entitled to due process rights if they can prove that they have a liberty interest. A liberty interest is attained if the grounds for the negative reappointment, promotion, or tenure decision affects their good name or reputation in the academic community or imposes on them a "stigma" or "disability" that prevents them from obtaining employment elsewhere. In these situations, the faculty member would be entitled to certain due process rights before the decision is finalized.

Due Process rights do not guarantee tenure, promotion, or reappointment, but these rights ensure that faculty members receive fair treatment. In the academic-employment domain, these rights include a statement of the reasons for nonrenewal, notice of the names and nature of the testimony of witnesses, an opportunity to be heard within a reasonable amount of time, and a hearing before impartial members of the institution who possess some academic expertise (Hustoles 1992).

The Supreme Court established the criteria for whether untenured faculty members in public institutions have due process rights in *Board of Regents of State Colleges vs. Roth* (1972) and *Perry vs. Sindermann* (1972). Essentially, the Supreme Court determined that untenured faculty members are entitled to due process rights when they have a "property interest," which is established by the contract of employment or state law; or a "liberty interest," which occurs when charges made against them impose a "stigma" or "disability" that prevents them from obtaining other employment.

Board of Regents of State Colleges vs. Roth (1972)
David Roth had been hired as an assistant professor of political science at Wisconsin State University-Oshkosh for a fixed term of one year. He was not rehired after his contract had expired and given no reasons for the decision or an appeal. A state law provided that faculty members were eligible for tenure after four years of continued service.

Roth sued, alleging that the university violated his 14th Amendment right to due process. The Supreme Court ruled that Roth did not have a right to a hearing or a statement of reasons because he had neither a liberty nor property interest in his employment.

The court held that the 14th Amendment protects faculty members' interests in "specific benefits." To have an interest in a specific benefit, the court reasoned, faculty members must be legally entitled to it; simply having an "abstract need or desire for it" is not enough. Property interests, the court indicated, are created and defined by existing rules or understandings that originate from state law, contracts, or the practices of the institution. In Roth's case, his employment was to terminate at the end of the academic year, and renewal was not automatic. According to the court's reasoning, only tenured professors have property interests guaranteeing constitutional due process rights. Nontenured faculty members, on the other hand, must look to employment contracts for any procedural rights.

Liberty interests under the 14th Amendment also are guaranteed due process protection. These interests are created when a public institution makes charges against a faculty member that might seriously damage his or her reputation or standing in the academic community or impose on the faculty member a "stigma or other disability" that prevents him or her from taking advantage of other employment opportunities. In Roth's case, the court held that he had not shown that nonrenewal imposed such a stigma or disability, perhaps failing to take into account the potential effect on his reputation as a result of a negative employment decision. The court noted that had the board of regents prevented Roth from seeking employment at other state universities, then he might have been able to claim that the state deprived him of a liberty interest without affording him due process.

Perry vs. Sindermann (1972)
Robert Sindermann had been employed as a professor by the Texas state college system for 10 consecutive years. After teaching for two years at the University of Texas and four years at San Antonio Junior College, he became a professor of government and social science at Odessa Junior College, where he remained employed for four consecutive

years. While thus employed, he publicly disagreed with the board of regents on a number of issues. After the series of 10 one-year contracts, the board of regents decided not to rehire him.

Like Roth, Sindermann was given neither an official reason for the nonrenewal nor an opportunity for a hearing, which he alleged violated his right to due process. He also alleged that he was released because of his political activities. The Supreme Court held that Sindermann had raised a genuine claim to de facto tenure which, if proved, would give him a property interest protected by the 14th Amendment. Sindermann had claimed that the college had a de facto tenure program, and he offered as proof the following statement in the faculty handbook:

> *Odessa College has no tenure system. The administration of the college wishes the faculty member to feel that he has permanent tenure as long as his teaching services are satisfactory and as long as he displays a cooperative attitude toward his co-workers and his superiors, and as long as he is happy in his work.*

The court held that Sindermann must be given an opportunity to prove that he had a legitimate claim of entitlement to continued employment in light of the policies and practices of the institution. Institutional practices and policies can be found in written contracts, the court indicated, but they also may be implied. The court held that Sindermann, employed for 10 years in the Texas higher-education system, might be able to show from the circumstances of his employment and other facts that there is an "unwritten common law" at his institution that certain faculty members have the equivalent of tenure.

Roth and *Sindermann* make it clear that the Constitution does not create property or liberty interests; these interests must derive from tort law (defamation, for example), contract law (the actual words of the contract or the practices of the institution, for example), or state law. While faculty members have the burden of proving that they have a property (tenure or its equivalent) or liberty (that they have been defamed) interest, once they do the institutions must establish valid grounds for dismissing them (Brown and Kurland 1993).

Property interests

As indicated, faculty members have a "property interest" in their employment, precipitating the need for due process, if they have a "legitimate expectation of continued employment*." This legal principle is easy to understand in the abstract, but it often is difficult to apply. Institutions do not always know when their policies or practices give faculty members a legitimate expectation of continued employment, and courts have not consistently applied the Supreme Court's decision. It is always prudent to put reappointment, promotion, and tenure policies and procedures in writing, and they should be adhered to. These materials also should be clear, consistent, and available to all faculty members.

As noted, due process requirements apply only to public institutions because they are subject to constitutional requirements. But private institutions do well to follow these guidelines in establishing their procedures because when the institutions policies are fair, courts will uphold their decisions. due process procedures can help the institution avoid or correct mistakes, protect academic freedom, foster faculty confidence, and resolve disputes in-house rather than by courts (Kaplin 1985).

Tenure policies should be clear. In *Olson vs. Idaho State University* (1994), also discussed in Section Two, an electronics instructor sued the university after he was denied tenure, alleging a violation of his due process rights. Olson had been employed in a series of five one-year contracts and he became eligible for tenure in his fifth year. His application was rejected by the president after he was recommended for tenure by the tenure committee, his department chairperson, and the dean. Olson claimed he had a property interest and thus continued employment because he had done all that was required and he was recommended by everyone except the president. The court, in upholding the university's decision, looked to the faculty handbook, which explicitly stated that tenure decisions must be approved by the board of trustees. Since the president rejected the recommendation of tenure and thereby withheld it from the board, not all the steps required for tenure were taken. As an untenured faculty member he was enti-

---

*Tenured faculty members have legitimate expectation of continued employment, of course. Untenured faculty members have such expectations while their contracts are in effect.

tled to a year's notice of nonrenewal, which the university provided.

As *Olson* illustrates, courts generally are unwilling to find that untenured faculty members have a property interest in continued employment if there are written procedures governing how tenure is acquired. Furthermore, courts rarely will interfere in the institution's interpretation of the criteria established for reappointment, promotion, or tenure. In *Colburn vs. Trustees of Indiana University* (1990), two faculty members sued the university for denial of tenure, promotion, and reappointment, alleging a violation of due process. They were hired in 1979 and continuously reappointed until 1985. They claimed that they were entitled to tenure, or at least reappointment, because they satisfied the written criteria for promotion and tenure and that they understood that reappointment would continue through the probationary period if their performance was satisfactory. They claimed that reappointment decisions were fairly automatic for employees in tenure-track positions. The court rejected their arguments, holding that the written criteria are mere guidelines rather than directives; as such, they do not substantially limit the institutions' discretion to determine who should receive tenure or reappointment.

....courts rarely will interfere in the institution's interpretation of the criteria established for reappointment, promotion, or tenure.

Although the faculty members in *Colburn* lost the case, the court indicated that where the institution's custom or practice made reappointment decisions automatic on satisfactory performance, a property interest may exist even if there are written policies governing these decisions. Nevertheless, the court determined that the faculty member's arguments were "weak." Generally, the court indicated, the written criteria for promotion or tenure are subjective and do not guarantee automatic renewals.

The court in *Colburn* indicated that an institution's written procedures do not limit its discretion. This principle also was illustrated in *Lovelace vs. Southeastern Massachusetts University* (1986). Lovelace's contract was not renewed, and he was not provided with a hearing. He sued, alleging that his due process rights were violated. He argued that the Board of Trustees/Faculty Federation Agreement was incorporated by reference into his contract, and this agreement guaranteed that he would not be denied reappointment without "justification." The agreement specified the criteria for reappointment and tenure and stated that in the "development of all recommendations for reappointment or nonreappointment justification of all recommendations must be included" (p. 421).

The university's policy also provided that although the president makes the final decision in reappointment cases, the board may review the decision and take further action. The court held that the university's officials did not lose their discretion to make decisions despite the language specifying "justification." This language, the court indicted, merely facilitated the president's decision by ensuring that he had the opinion of the relevant constituents before making his decisions; it did not imply any other rights.

Since the institution's written policies do not limit its discretion in employment matters, oral assurances are even less likely to form the basis of property interests. In *Lovelace*, the faculty member also alleged that after receiving notice of his nonrenewal, he was informed by the president (through the dean) that if his student evaluations improved he would be renewed after the spring semester. His evaluations improved, but he was not renewed. The court held that where a college has written, formalized procedures for reappointment, a faculty member cannot claim that he or she somehow had acquired an expectation of employment because of oral assurances. The president's words, the court believed, only indicated that he would be the judge of whether the faculty member showed sufficient improvement warranting renewal.

Other courts have indicated that oral assurances, if enough and combined with written ones, may give faculty members a legitimate expectation of continued employment. In *Soni vs. Board of Trustees of the University of Tennessee* (1975), discussed previously, the court held that oral and written assurances made to the faculty by the department head gave the plaintiff a reasonable expectation that he would be tenured, even though there was a formal tenure process. Soni had been promised by the department chairperson that he would be tenured if he became a U.S. citizen, and he was assured that he was "wanted" and that his "prospects were good." He also was permitted to enroll in the university's pension plan. The result of this case, however, was probably based on the extent, and particular nature, of the assurances. Mere oral promises, without more, will not create "property interests."

Soni notwithstanding, courts are extremely reluctant to find that a faculty member has a legitimate claim of continued employment if written procedures governing tenure exist. Assurances by key administrators or fluctuations from institutional policies do not, generally, seem to convince courts that untenured faculty members have property interests in their employment, thus requiring their institutions to provide due process before nonrenewing their contracts. Some courts are not even swayed when there is some evidence that the negative decision may have been based upon illegal factors. In *King vs. Board of Regents of University of Wisconsin System* (1990), a female faculty member hired as an assistant professor in the School of Allied Health Professions at the University of Wisconsin-Milwaukee sued after unanimously being denied tenure. She alleged that she was sexually harassed by the assistant dean of the School of Allied Health Professions and the director of the occupational-therapy program and that the reasons for the adverse employment decision were gender discrimination and retaliation for her charges of sexual harassment. The court held that as an untenured faculty member she did not have a property interest in continued employment. Furthermore, although the court found that she was verbally assaulted, fondled, and physically attacked by the assistant dean, she had to prove that the adverse employment decision was based on discriminatory motivations such as sexual harassment and retaliation for her exercise of constitutionally protected rights. The court did not find evidence that the assistant dean had been involved in the tenure decision, and there was no evidence of discriminatory motivation by the director.

De facto tenure

The Supreme Court opened the door for de facto tenure claims in *Perry vs. Sindermann* (1972). Faculty members may be able to claim that they have tenure or some form of indefinite employment if they can establish that institutional rules or understandings between themselves and their institutions have created a legitimate expectation to continued employment. Courts, however, generally are unwilling to determine that faculty members have de facto tenure where there are formal, clear, and explicit tenure policies, and these policies are adhered to.

In *Omlor vs. Cleveland State University* (1989), the court rejected the faculty member's claim to de facto tenure because the institution's policies clearly indicated that tenure decisions must be approved by the board of trustees. Omlor, a faculty member in the business college, was first hired as a part-time instructor in 1969 and appointed to full-time instructor in 1972. Tenure at the university was governed by a formal written policy which provided that tenure would be granted by formal action of the board of trustees.

Since 1972, Omlor received a series of seven full-time contracts. His contracts stated that the probationary period should not exceed seven years and that failure to qualify for tenure by the conclusion of the probationary period disqualified a faculty member from further employment at the university. The first few contracts stated that his tenure status would be determined by June 1978, but his later contracts indicated that the decision would be made by January 1978. He was informed on May 26, 1978, that the next contract would be terminal. Omlor had been considered for tenure pursuant to the university's tenure policy. He was recommended for tenure by the department chairperson and the dean of the business college but rejected by the college's tenure committee. The board of trustees voted against tenure. Omlor claimed that he had attained de facto tenure based on the series of contracts indicating that a decision would be made by January 1978 and on the fact that he worked for three years before he became eligible for tenure (giving him more than seven years of service).

The court held that the weight of authority regarding de facto tenure supported the university's contention that an untenured faculty member has no entitlement to tenure on a de facto basis, where the university has a formal tenure system providing for the granting of tenure by the board of trustees. Although tenure need not always be acquired through formal procedures, the court stated, it must be based on the mutually explicit understanding of the practices and customs of the institution. The three contracts indicating that the tenure decision would be forthcoming on or before Jan. 15, 1978, did not change Omlor's tenure rights under the policy nor did his service prior to his appointment to full-time status.

Perhaps another court might have held differently in

Omlor by finding that any faculty member employed beyond the probationary period is entitled to tenure by default (see *Beckwith vs. Rhode Island School of Design* 1979). Nevertheless, *Omlor* illustrates the reluctance of the courts to bind an institution to a tenure appointment where the written policies are explicit as to how tenure is acquired.

On the other hand, courts have not always been consistent in their rulings on de facto tenure. In *Jones vs. University of Central Oklahoma* (1993), the court found that an untenured faculty member may have a legitimate claim to continued employment despite the existence of a formal tenure policy. Jones sued the university alleging that his due process rights were violated when he was denied tenure. The university argued that he was denied tenure because he failed to satisfy the formalized 19-step process used to evaluate tenure applications. Jones argued that the university's past practices and representations entitled him to be evaluated under an informal and less strenuous "local tenure" process, which considers longevity, does not require a formal application, and "where tenure is awarded as a matter of course."

The court held that a legitimate claim of "entitlement to tenure" in the state is defined solely through the application of state contract and employment law. If under contract or employment law faculty members established an implied right to continued employment through alleged unwritten "local tenure" procedures, they have a property interest protected by the due process clause of the 14th Amendment, even where there are written procedures governing tenure. Jones, the court held, was entitled to prove that he had attained tenure through unwritten "local tenure" procedures. As the Supreme Court indicated in *Perry vs. Sindermann,* if an action by the institution creates the expectation of employment, the faculty member is entitled to due process to determine whether he or she has tenure. *Jones* is an illustration of what can happen when an institution fails to follow its written policies. Had the university done so, it would have prevailed.

The *Jones* ruling is an exception to courts' general refusal to allow faculty members to prove de facto tenure where the institutions have a formal tenure policy. But as indicated throughout this report, institutions that do not wish to become involved in such lawsuits should develop formal, clear, explicit, and widely distributed tenure procedures and follow them.

Liberty interests

Even though *Roth* and *Sindermann* indicated that certain dismissals would implicate liberty interests (that is, when the faculty member's reputation is threatened, affecting his or her ability to obtain other positions), the Supreme Court has made it difficult to establish such an interest in academic-employment decisions. In *Bishop vs. Wood* (1976), a police officer who had been discharged and orally informed of the reasons in a private meeting sued, claiming a denial of due process. Regarding liberty interests, the court held that charges communicated in private to the employee cannot form the basis for a deprivation of a liberty interest, even if the charges are false. This decision is important in the faculty-employment context, in that decisions, and the reasons for them, rarely are made public.

Peer-review information generally is confidential, but there are situations in which this kind of information may be disclosed or made public (at public institutions subject to "open records" laws, for example). In these situations, a faculty member may be able to show that the charges made against him or her implicated liberty interests, thus requiring the institution to provide due process rights (an opportunity to be heard or to challenge witnesses). Charges of dishonesty, immorality, or professional incompetence are examples of "stigmas" preventing the faculty member from obtaining other employment. Public institutions should be careful about the reasons they give, to whom they communicate the reasons, and the evidence on which they rely in reappointment, promotion, or tenure decisions. They also should provide a hearing or some opportunity to be heard on any allegations that may damage a faculty member's reputation.

Some courts have refused to hold that the faculty member's liberty interests were implicated in a negative employment decision when no reasons are given. In *Olson vs. Idaho State University* (1994), discussed previously, the faculty member also alleged that he was not granted tenure because of charges of insubordination, and these charges implicated his liberty interests, entitling him to a hearing before he was dismissed. The court held that since no reasons were given for the decision against him, Olson could not claim that his liberty interests were violated. This decision is consistent with *Bishop vs. Wood* (1976), which held that charges that are not made public cannot form the basis for liberty-interests claims.

Although the university prevailed in *Olson*, it is wise to provide reasons for the decision. And if the decision is based upon potentially defamatory charges, the institution would be in sound legal (and moral) standing if it provides the faculty member with an opportunity to challenge the decision. Providing faculty members with an opportunity to contest the allegations may not avoid a lawsuit, but courts will look favorably upon institutions that have fair procedures.

Freedom of Speech and Academic Freedom

Untenured faculty members have limited, if any, due process rights in job renewals. This does not mean that they have no other constitutional rights. Faculty members may not be denied reappointment, promotion, or tenure as a punishment for their exercise of First Amendment rights. And as we will discuss in Section Four, faculty members at public institutions also have a constitutional right not to be discriminated against on the basis of race or gender or any other illegal motive.

First Amendment rights include freedom of speech, freedom of expression, and freedom of religion. Faculty members are entitled to academic freedom, which encompasses all such freedoms. These freedoms become "constitutional" at public institutions. The right to speak freely on any matter goes by the name "academic freedom" when exercised in the context of a faculty member's teaching, research, or service duties. Academic freedom is not specifically mentioned in the First Amendment or anywhere else in the Constitution. The Supreme Court has held, however, that academic freedom is "a special concern of the First Amendment" (*Keyishian vs. Board of Regents* 1967). Faculty members and institutions have academic freedom rights, and their rights may conflict on occasion. Institutions have an academic freedom right to determine "who shall teach," and faculty members have an academic freedom right not to be punished for what they say or how they express themselves. There are, of course, limits to these rights, and these limits are the focus of this section.

First Amendment rights apply at public institutions. Many public and private institutions, however, have incorporated the AAUP's academic freedom principles into their employment contracts. Faculty members' academic freedom rights at private institutions, therefore, may be protected by contract. There also has been a recent trend toward incorporating academic freedom principles in collective-bargaining agreements or other organized labor activity (Olivas 1989). Furthermore, state law also may provide freedom-of-speech or academic freedom rights to faculty members at both private and public institutions.

History of legal recognition of academic freedom
The notion of academic freedom can be traced to 19th-century Germany, where the concepts of *lehrfreiheit* (freedom of teaching) and *lernfreiheit* (freedom of learning) were practiced. Even though courts rarely overturned employment decisions, campus conflicts over evolutionary science and populist economics helped the profession persuade governing boards not to punish faculty members for their research findings and to grant tenure to protect academic freedom (Metzger 1993b).

As a result of the McCarthy era, the legal basis of academic freedom was expanded by constitutional law and contract law (Metzger 1993b). The Supreme Court first moved toward recognizing academic freedom as a constitutional issue in *Meyer vs. Nebraska* (1923), when the court struck down a state law prohibiting foreign-language instruction in private schools (Van Alstyne 1993b). The concept of judicially recognized academic freedom was further developed in *Sweezy vs. New Hampshire* (1957). In *Sweezy*, the court overturned the contempt conviction of Paul Sweezy, who refused to disclose what he discussed in a class lecture and his knowledge of communist-party activity in the state. Although the court focused on whether Sweezy had been denied due process, not academic freedom, the majority opinion noted that teachers and students "must always remain free to inquire, to study and to evaluate, to gain new maturity and understanding; otherwise our civilization will stagnate and die" (p. 250).

Justice Felix Frankfurter, in a famous concurring opinion, defended academic freedom. He wrote that "when weighed against the grave harm resulting from governmental intrusion into the intellectual life of a university," the government's justification that it wanted to prevent subversive activities is inadequate (p. 261). The university, Frankfurter noted, provided:

> that atmosphere which is most conducive to speculation, experiment and creation. It is an atmosphere in which there prevail "the four essential freedoms" of a university — to determine for itself on academic grounds who may teach, what may be taught, how it shall be taught, and who may be admitted to study... (pp. 262-3).

The Supreme Court reinforced academic freedom's protection by the First Amendment in *Keyishian vs. Board of Regents* (1967), when the court struck down New York's loyalty laws and regulations. Justice William Brennan wrote:

> Our Nation is deeply committed to safeguarding academic freedom, which is of transcendent value to all of us and not merely to the teachers concerned. That freedom is therefore a special concern of the First Amendment, which does not tolerate laws that cast a pall of orthodoxy over the classroom (pp. 603).

Although *Sweezy* and *Keyishian* both involved individual faculty members, the language of the court refers to both individual and institutional academic freedom. Two other cases specifically give institutions academic freedom rights: *University of California Regents vs. Bakke* (1978) and *Regents of the University of Michigan vs. Ewing* (1985). In *Bakke*, the Supreme Court invalidated particular elements of the university's affirmative-action admissions policy, but Powell wrote that the university's concern about a diverse student body involves a First Amendment interest. Institutions, therefore, may use race as one factor in admissions decisions. His defense of educational diversity was an acknowledgment and defense of the academic freedom of an institution (Poch 1993).

In *Ewing*, the Supreme Court upheld the university's refusal to allow a student to retake a test he had failed and the subsequent dismissal of the student from a university program. The court held that when dealing with "academic decisions, judges should show great respect for professional judgment" (p. 225). In these cases, the Supreme Court justices supported institutional academic freedom and established it as a value protected by the First Amendment.

Untenured faculty members and academic freedom

Academic freedom has been the subject of much discussion and analysis (Poch 1993; Van Alstyne 1993a). It also is one of the most sacred of the faculty members' rights. Contemporary academic freedom issues include: artistic expression through visual modes such as paintings, drawings, photographs, motion pictures, plays, and sculptures; political correctness; hate speech; and academic freedom in church-related colleges and universities (Poch 1993). Higher education institutions also have asserted an academic freedom privilege to protect peer-review information from disclosure. We will treat this matter in greater detail in Section Six.

Although academic freedom has been discussed as a constitutional right, the legal boundaries of academic freedom also are shaped by the contract of employment; faculty members possess whatever academic freedom is guaranteed under their contracts (Kaplin and Lee 1995). Courts, however, will uphold academic freedom as a constitutional right when the government attempts to control the content of the university or faculty member's speech. Therefore, the faculty member's rights against the institution are defined primarily through contract law. The institution and faculty member's rights against the government are defined primarily through constitutional law. And because faculty members at public institutions are state employees, they, too, have First Amendment rights that must be protected by their institutions.

As discussed previously, many institutions incorporate the 1940 Statement of Principles in the faculty contract, and this statement is considered the most important policy statement on academic freedom. Even if the statement is not explicitly incorporated into the contract, courts have referred to the statement as evidence of academic custom and practice. Institutions should determine whether, or to what extent, they wish to incorporate the statement into their contracts. Any intent to exclude this document from the contract should be explicitly and unambiguously indicated.

The 1940 Statement of Principles on Academic Freedom

and Tenure states that during the probationary period a teacher should have the same level of academic freedom as all other faculty members (AAUP 1990). Specifically, the statement defines academic freedom as the freedom to research and to publish the results of the research; the freedom to discuss the faculty member's subject in the classroom (but controversial matter should be relevant to the subject); and the freedom to speak or write freely as a citizen.

Individual faculty members and institutions have academic freedom rights, and these rights sometimes may conflict. Faculty members who ask courts to adjudicate claims that their institutions have violated their academic freedom may find that the institutions counter by asserting that any judicial resolution of these claims amounts to state intervention in institutional affairs, thereby violating the institutions' academic freedom rights (Rabban 1993). All of these cases, therefore, illustrate how courts balance these conflicting rights.

The results of these cases usually depend on the type of speech involved. The outcome of a case, for example, may depend on whether the speech is exercised in the classroom or in the faculty member's private activities. A faculty member may speak freely about matters of public concern, but what if the speech negatively affects the legitimate interests of the institution? The remainder of this section addresses these issues in greater detail.

Academic freedom in the classroom

Institutions have the greatest amount of discretion concerning what occurs in the classroom, course content, and pedagogy, and courts are extremely reluctant to get involved in those matters (Poch 1993). In addition, institutional discretion to make curricular decisions, hire employees on the "basis of their philosophical bent," eliminate or reduce programs, and elevate classroom performance has been protected on the basis of academic freedom (Metzger 1993b, pp. 7-8).

In *Lovelace vs. Southeastern Massachusetts University* (1986), discussed previously, the faculty member alleged that he was not rehired because he advocated strict academic standards, and he refused to lower grading standards in his courses following several requests from admin-

The 1940 Statement of Principles on Academic Freedom and Tenure states that during the probationary period a teacher should have the same level of academic freedom as all other faculty members.

istrators that he do so. Although the court assumed that Lovelace's refusal to lower grading standards was a motivating factor in the decision not to reappoint him, the court held that a professor's grading policy was not unconditionally protected by the Constitution. To hold that it was, the court indicated, would constrict the university in defining and performing its educational mission.

Therefore, it appears that institutions have an academic freedom interest in determining what should be taught, how it should be taught, and when it should be taught. One reason for courts' reluctance to interfere in these matters has to do with institutions' right to protect students from certain types of speech. For example, institutions may protect students from profanity and obscenity in the classroom. Another reason lies with judges' beliefs that they do not have the requisite professional expertise to substitute their judgments for those of administrators, who are professionally trained to make such judgments, and who have been publicly entrusted with the responsibility of making these types of decisions.

There are limits to institutions' ability to punish faculty members for the content of their speech. Courts will not uphold negative employment decisions that were motivated by the faculty member's exercise of First Amendment rights. Some speech, though arguably offensive, is protected and cannot be censored easily. In *Dube vs. State University of New York* (1990), the court determined that a faculty member of African studies raised legitimate concerns when he claimed he was denied promotion and tenure for teaching a course in which he claimed that Nazism, Apartheid, and Zionism were three forms of racism. The court determined that his beliefs were protected by the First Amendment, and a jury should decide whether his dismissal was based on the exercise of protected rights.

As illustrated in *Dube*, some speech, though offensive, may be protected by the First Amendment. Institutions may not punish a faculty member for exercising protected speech, even if the speech is racist, disruptive, or otherwise violates institutional values. In *Levin vs. Harleston* (1991), for example, a tenured professor in the philosophy department at City College publicly stated that African-Americans were less intelligent than whites and that African-Americans could only succeed when academic standards were lowered.

As a result of his controversial words, angry students disrupted his classes, but the administration did not take action against the disrupting students. After setting up a committee to determine whether Levin's speech went beyond academic freedom and became "conduct unbecoming a faculty member," the administration decided to allow students who felt uncomfortable in Levin's course to switch to a parallel section. Between one-third and one-half of the students who normally would have registered for Levin's course opted for the parallel section during the next few semesters. Levin sued City College and its officials because he believed this move (the parallel section) singled him out on ideological, not pedagogical, grounds in violation of his civil rights and the First and 14th amendments.

The federal district court held that City College officials had sought to punish Levin for his speech. The court prohibited the college from taking any disciplinary action against Levin or maintaining the parallel section. The court also ordered the administration to take reasonable steps to prevent the disruption of his classes. A federal appeals court affirmed the lower court's decision on all matters except that the college had to take reasonable steps to prevent the disruption of Levin's classes (*Levin vs. Harleston* 1992).

In addition to a faculty member's beliefs, a professor's evaluation of students' work also may be protected by the First Amendment. In *Parate vs. Isibor* (1989), for example, the appeals court reversed a lower court's dismissal of a faculty member's claim that his First Amendment rights were violated. Parate, an untenured associate professor in the civil engineering department at Tennessee State University, established a numerical grading scale for a course he taught. Two students complained to Parate about their final grade, and Parate agreed to change one student's grade but not the other's.

The dean of the School of Engineering and Technology instructed Parate to change his grading scale so both students would receive a higher grade. Parate initially refused, but after constant pressure from the dean and department head he finally agreed. For the next couple of years, the dean and department head challenged Parate's grading in other courses, criticized his teaching methods, gave him unfavorable performance evaluations, refused to reimburse him for authorized travel expenses, and impeded his research efforts. In March 1985, Parate was informed by the president that his contract would not be renewed for a fourth year. Parate attempted reconciliation with the dean, who informed him that his contract would be renewed but "you must obey and never disobey your dean" (p. 825).

In September 1985, a few students challenged the grades they received in Parate's classes, disrupted his classes, and threatened to complain to the dean. A couple of days later, the dean and department head appeared in Parate's class unannounced, disrupted his class, and berated him in front of his students. At one point, they ordered him to "stop the roll" and complete a problem on the blackboard without addressing the students. The dean later relieved Parate of his teaching duties. Parate sued, alleging, among other issues, violations of his academic freedom under the First Amendment.

Although the court emphasized the importance of judicial deference in academic matters, it held that the assignment of a letter grade could be considered a communicative act entitled to constitutional protection, and an institution that forces a faculty member to change a previously assigned grade may violate the First Amendment. The court indicated that administrators had the option of changing such a grade through administrative channels. The behavior of the administrators in this case also may have influenced the court's decision.

Faculty members also have the right to engage in political activities, and they must prove that a negative reappointment, promotion, or tenure decision was motivated by the faculty member's speech. In *Cooper vs. Ross* (1979), an untenured assistant professor of history at the University of Arkansas was informed that he would not be reappointed after he became a member of the Communist Party and after he informed his classes that he taught from a Marxist point of view. Although the university provided other reasons for the nonreappointment, the court believed that the decision was substantially motivated by the fact that the faculty member was a Communist, and this type of association was protected by the First Amendment. The university failed to show that the decision would have been the same irrespective of Cooper's exercise of his constitutional rights.

Academic freedom in institutional or public affairs

When the faculty member's speech relates to public or institutional matters or concerns, courts have been less willing to defer to the institution's judgment. The Supreme Court in *Pickering vs. Board of Education* (1968) held that teachers have a First Amendment right to comment on matters of public concern, and the public institution must prove that it has compelling interest in prohibiting such speech. The court held that public-school teachers have a First Amendment right to speak out on matters of public interest in connection with the operations of the public schools in which they work, and only a legitimate state interest would justify any prohibition of the teacher's speech.

Metzger argued that *Pickering* was both a victory for academic freedom and a loss (1993b). On one hand, *Pickering* held that faculty members' constitutional rights must be protected. On the other hand, it also required that faculty members prove that their speech is a matter of public concern, and institutions would prevail if they are able to show that the faculty members' words impaired legitimate interests such as the harmonious work relationships necessary to promote their educational missions, or they are disruptive (p. 7).

The issue for many courts, therefore, is whether the faculty member's speech or expression relates to a public matter, and speech classified as "public concern" is strongly protected. Certain racist speech may not be regarded as a matter of legitimate public concern. For example, in *Omlor vs. Cleveland State University* (1989), discussed previously, the faculty member allegedly made a remark that a certain person was "good guy, for a Jew. I like about 40 percent of the Jewish people I meet." The court held that Omlor could not claim these remarks were constitutionally protected because the words were not "a matter of legitimate public concern," and even if the president considered his remark in his decision not to recommend tenure, the decision was proper.

The faculty member's political activities are a legitimate matter of public concern and may not be used to deny reappointment, promotion, or tenure. In *Goss vs. San Jacinto Junior College* (1979), a faculty member claimed her contract was not renewed because of her political and union activities, which were protected by the First Amendment. The college claimed that Goss was not rehired because of declining enrollments and poor work. The court held that there was ample evidence that Goss had not been rehired because of her political and union activities. Institutions that prove evidence that the decision was made on legitimate academic grounds (such as inadequate scholarship or poor teaching), however, likely will prevail in these types of cases.

As *Goss* illustrated, courts are suspicious of institutional actions that appear to coincide with the faculty member's exercise of protected speech. In *Roos vs. Smith* (1993), an untenured faculty member of education at Jackson State University sued after not being reappointed for what she claimed was a violation of her First Amendment rights. Roos alleged that her contract was not renewed after she testified on behalf of another white faculty member in a Title VII race discrimination suit against the university (see Section Four). She testified at that lawsuit, in essence, that whites were unwelcome at Jackson State University. She received notice of nonrenewal less than a month later.

The court held that as an untenured faculty member Roos had no entitlement to continued employment at the university, and so her contract need not have been renewed for any reason or no reason at all unless the reason for that action infringed upon her constitutionally protected rights. Her testimony in the discrimination case was protected by the First Amendment. Although the university claimed that to receive accreditation of one of the school of education's doctoral programs it needed to release Roos and hire a professor with appropriate qualifications, the court determined that the university's reasons were a pretext for illegally infringing upon her First Amendment rights.

Faculty members at public institutions have a First Amendment right to express themselves on matters of public concern. Institutions, however, may restrict speech that interferes with its educational objectives. This appears simple; in reality, balancing the right to speak on matters of public concern with the institutions' right to conduct their missions is difficult. Furthermore, a recent Supreme Court case implied that in disciplining faculty members for activities that are alleged to implicate First Amendment interests, institutions may have to conduct reasonable investigations, and faculty members may not be disciplined until the institutions have substantiated the allegations (see *Waters vs. Churchill* 1994).

Academic freedom in private life

Faculty members enjoy the most protection in matters relating to their private lives. Courts are reluctant to uphold institutional restriction of faculty members' speech in matters involving their private lives. Faculty members do not lose their rights as private citizens simply because they work in public institutions. They may comment on public issues, associate with whom they please, or otherwise express themselves as private citizens. Courts have held for faculty members who chose not to abide by an institution's grooming regulations (see *Hander vs. San Jacinto Junior College* 1975); faculty members who held outside jobs (see *Trister vs. University of Mississippi* 1969); and faculty members who spoke on controversial matters (see *Jeffries vs. Harleston* 1993*; *Levin vs. Harleston* 1991).

This right, however, is not absolute. The 1940 Statement of Principles, for example, requires that faculty members should "at all times be accurate, should exercise appropriate restraint, should show respect for the opinions of others, and should make every effort to indicate that [he or she] is not an institutional [spokesperson]" (AAUP 1990). Institutions, therefore, may be able to frame a legal argument that would allow them to restrict the private activities of faculty members if they prove that these activities interfere with the faculty members' teaching or other legitimate institutional interests (Kaplin and Lee 1995).

Eastern State University Scenario

Your claim to tenure is based upon statements made in the faculty handbook, which is part of your contract. Essentially, the handbook indicates that after six years a faculty member either has tenure or is to be dismissed. The univer-

---

*The Jeffries case has been long and controversial. When the City College of New York removed Professor Jeffries from a departmental chairmanship for his controversial speech, the courts ruled in his favor. Later, the Supreme Court vacated the lower courts' rulings and sent the case back to be reconsidered. The appeals court later held that the institution did not violate the professor's First Amendment rights because it was motivated by a reasonable prediction of the professor's disruption of the institution's operations.

---

sity also incorporated into its contracts the 1940 Statement of Principles, which states that any full-time faculty member has tenure after seven years (see Section Two).

You have been employed full time for seven years. Courts, however, are extremely reluctant to determine that faculty members have tenure when there are explicit policies governing how tenure is acquired. The handbook states that tenure is not automatic and that the board of trustees must confer tenure. It is unlikely that you will prevail in this matter because the board has not approved tenure. Furthermore, your constitutional claims to due process will not be vindicated if a court determines that you do not have tenure or at least a "legitimate claim to continued employment." But even if a court believed your claims are valid, the Constitution entitles you to due process, not continuous employment. Eastern State University need only provide you with certain procedural rights, including a right to an impartial hearing, which many institutions provide as matter of course.

Your claims that the negative decision was motivated by your criticisms of the university may be valid if you have some evidence that this, in fact, is true. Was the decision to deny you tenure made soon after your criticisms? Is there other evidence that the institution was motivated by these criticisms? If so, your First Amendment rights are at stake because institutions may not punish faculty members for speaking on matters of public concern, and your speech would certainly qualify as one of "public concern." Also, the university has contracted with you to provide you academic freedom rights (the 1940 Statement of Principles). Therefore, your public criticisms about institutional matters not only are protected by the First Amendment but also by your contract. The institution, however, still may be able to prove that its decision was not motivated by your speech but instead was based upon legitimate academic grounds (inadequate teaching and research, for example). But if you prove some evidence that Eastern State University's reasons for denying you tenure were a pretext, then you have a valid claim.

Summary
The Constitution protects the property interests of faculty members in public institutions. Property interests may not

be infringed on before institutions provide faculty members with due process, including adequate notice and a hearing. Untenured faculty members, however, do not have the right to due process after their contracts have expired unless the contract of employment or state law provides them with a legitimate expectation of continued employment. Courts usually are unwilling to find that faculty members have acquired tenure through informal means, especially if there are written and explicit policies governing how tenure is acquired.

All faculty members in public institutions are entitled to due process if their liberty interests are compromised. Liberty interests arise when institutions make charges or allegations against faculty members that may damage their reputations or impose a "stigma or other disability" preventing them from obtaining other employment. In negative reappointment, promotion, or tenure decisions, liberty interests are difficult to prove because the reasons for the denial are rarely made public — a required condition for prevailing in such a lawsuit.

Faculty members' academic freedom also is protected. But courts are reluctant to become involved in strict academic matters, such as pedagogy, grading, and course offerings, unless the institutions' decisions are intended to punish faculty members for their speech. Courts will become involved in negative employment decisions that are motivated by the faculty members' exercise of their First Amendment rights. These rights include the freedom to comment on matters of public or institutional concern, the freedom to speak and express oneself — even if such speech is considered offensive — and the freedom to engage in certain activities such as testifying in court cases or engaging in political or union activities.

While these First Amendment cases involve public institutions, and constitutional rights do not apply at private colleges and universities, all administrators should provide these rights because they ensure fairness and support academic values. academic freedom rights, especially, primarily are defined by the contract of employment. Courts reviewing such contract claims against private institutions may well base their decisions on reasoning established in constitutional cases.

EMPLOYMENT DISCRIMINATION

Consider these scenarios:

Professor Y, an African-American, male faculty member in the social science department of Private University, has been denied tenure. The university makes the following claims: Professor Y's scholarship is weak (he has very few publications); his research interests are inconsistent with the goal of the department; and colleagues and students have claimed that he is "hard to get along with." Professor Y makes the following claims: He has sufficient publications; he has heard some of his colleagues make "racist" remarks against him; he is the only African-American in his department and no African-American has ever been tenured in his department; and white professors have been tenured with fewer publications. The department and university tenure committees voted in his favor by a slight margin, but the dean and the academic vice president recommended against tenure.

Professor X, a white, female faculty member in the School of Education at Public University, has been denied promotion to full professor. Professor X has published numerous articles and one book based on her dissertation. The university claimed she was denied promotion because she had not published a second book. All full professors had published at least two books (although some do not have as many articles as Professor X). Professor X makes the following claims: She was informed by her department chair that she need not publish a second book; she was informed by her chair and several colleagues that her numerous articles counted for "at least two books," since it may be more difficult for women to develop the informal networks and professional and personal relationships crucial for the publication of any book, the two-book requirement "in effect bars the vast majority of women from full professorships." While more than half of the School of Education is composed of women faculty members, there are no female full professors.

What legal bases do Professors Y and X have for their claims of discrimination? What would a court

---

decide? Assuming that the professors initiate litigation and win, what should be the remedy?

The reappointment, promotion, and tenure process can be conducive to illegal discrimination. The criteria used often are vaguely defined and subjectively applied, and faculty members subjected to negative employment decisions usually are given very few reasons, except perhaps that their teaching, scholarship, or service was generally inadequate. Furthermore, these decisions often are made in closed meetings, and evaluators both inside and outside the institution are expected to keep their decisions confidential to encourage candor (LaNoue and Lee 1987; Leap 1993).

The primary difficulty in discrimination cases for faculty members is that reappointment, promotion, and tenure decisions almost always depend upon subjective attributes: creativity, rapport with colleagues and students, teaching ability, and many other intangible qualities that are difficult to measure (Leap 1993). Courts often have had difficulty determining whether inadequate performance or illegal discrimination caused the negative decision (LaNoue and Lee 1987), and they usually are unwilling to second-guess the appropriateness of the decision. In the majority of cases, courts will review the promotion and tenure procedures but not the substance of decisions, finding the latter within the discretion of the academic professionals (Hendrickson and Lee 1983).

Given its potential, there actually are very few reported cases of flagrant incidents of gender or race discrimination. There is, however, evidence of an antiminority and antiwoman sentiment in academia (Leap 1993). Women and faculty of color are seriously underrepresented among the tenured faculty ranks. In 1992, for example, only 61 African-American professors held endowed chairs in colleges and universities, and one-fifth of these professorships were located at the University of North Carolina at Chapel Hill (Leap 1993). Furthermore, women and faculty of color often have felt that they were never completely accepted in academia: They often were not sought for collaboration on research projects or curricular matters; they often were excluded from informal department communications and professional networking; and their research, unique teaching methods, and service to the community were not always rewarded (Leap 1993).

An increasing number of studies and literature reviews have indicated that women and faculty of color experience many challenges in academia. These works have emphasized the barriers to access and advancement (Johnsrud and Des Jarlais 1994; Menges and Exum 1983; Moody 1988; Reyes and Halcon 1991); strategies for recruitment and retention (Blackwell 1988; Mickelson and Oliver 1991); job satisfaction (Aguirre, Hernandez, and Martinez 1995); socialization (Pollard 1990; Tierney and Rhoads 1993); institutional racism (Anderson 1988; Reyes and Halcon 1988); the character and structure of the academic profession as hindering their success (Exum et al. 1984); and the differences in the experiences of faculty of color and white faculty (Johnsrud 1993). The general theme in these studies is that women and faculty of color face many challenges, and to be promoted and tenured they need more professional and personal support than they are receiving.

Because of serious underrepresentation; the barriers faced; and the nature of the reappointment, promotion, and tenure process, women and faculty of color increasingly are alleging illegal discrimination as the basis for negative employment decisions. Most faculty members alleging discrimination have lost their cases because judges generally have been unwilling to overturn the decisions made. But recent amendments to Title VII of the Civil Rights Act of 1964, which prohibits race and gender discrimination, may result in more victories for faculty members victimized by discrimination. Title VII now allows juries (as well as judges) to determine whether discrimination has occurred. Lee pointed out that this change may have led to a number of recent victories in discrimination cases probably because juries are less likely than judges to defer to academic expertise (1995). Understanding the issues involved in these cases is important because of the increase in this kind of litigation, the recent changes to Title VII, and the enormous impact of these cases on everyone involved.

Faculty members in employment-discrimination cases are more likely to prevail on procedural or jurisdictional issues than on the merits.

The Nature of Employment-Discrimination Litigation

Faculty members in employment-discrimination cases are more likely to prevail on procedural or jurisdictional issues than on the merits (LaNoue and Lee 1987). The most common case involves single, white females suing predominantly white institutions, but very few of these women have prevailed. Class-action suits brought by women have been more successful as are lawsuits by white faculty members against historically black institutions. African-Americans and other faculty of color almost always have lost their cases (LaNoue and Lee 1987)*.

Courts must necessarily examine the criteria actually used to determine whether illegal discrimination has occurred, and so they are less likely to automatically defer to academic expertise than in other cases (Lee 1985). Despite this, courts are reluctant to interfere in the internal affairs of colleges and universities[†]. Many courts have held that if the professional decision has an "adequate" factual basis for the conclusions reached, they will not substitute their judgments for the views of the relevant professionals (Rabban 1993). Courts have even upheld denials of reappointment, promotion, or tenure to those individuals whose research interests or temperaments do not fit in with other faculty members (Hendrickson and Lee 1983).

Courts generally have upheld academic decisions in which the process has been lengthy or has more than one level of review, even if institutions have failed to follow their own procedures (Lee 1985). They will rarely inquire into the accuracy or appropriateness of the criteria used to evaluate faculty members (LaNoue and Lee 1987). Where courts have evaluated the substance of decisions to determine whether discrimination has occurred they have focused on factors that are not unique to academia, such as the timing of the decision and quantitative or comparative data (Rabban 1993).

When looking into the substance of a decision, courts become suspicious of obviously weak, implausible, ambiguous, and poorly substantiated reasons. Courts also may become suspicious when a negative decision occurs despite the unanimous recommendation of faculty committees (Rabban 1993). In the few cases in which faculty members

---

*The study conducted by LaNoue and Lee (1987) involved cases that were resolved on either procedural or substantive issues. This information does not include cases that were settled out of court nor does it include those cases that were resolved within the institution.

[†]But recent legislation permitting employment discrimination cases to juries may result in more decisions on the merits. Judges are reluctant to interfere in these decisions, but juries are not as likely to defer to academic expertise in these matters.

have prevailed, the peer-review decision usually was positive but was overturned at higher administrative levels (Hendrickson and Lee 1983).

Consequences of Employment-Discrimination Litigation
Employment-discrimination cases are extremely complex and require a great amount of resources. The trials tend to be lengthy, sometimes covering weeks and producing thousands of pages of transcripts (Lee 1985). The evidence presented in these cases has included the deliberations of promotion and tenure committees and testimony from administrators (chairpersons, deans, vice presidents, and presidents), trustees, and outside evaluators. Faculty members who have been tenured or promoted may have their qualifications and abilities scrutinized publicly, as suing faculty members may need to prove that they were as able as those who did attain tenure (see *Chronicle of Higher Education*, Feb. 3, 1995). Institutions often have been required to present exhaustive evidence to establish that the decision and procedures were fair. Even if the institution prevails in the litigation, as often has been the case, the time, money, and good will lost in the process takes its toll on everyone (Lee 1985). The resources expended in preventing lawsuits also is great; continuously adding procedural or documentary requirements for decision-making can be costly (LaNoue and Lee 1987).

These cases also may have political and emotional consequences as well. For colleges and universities, these lawsuits provide a precedent (and perhaps incentive) for other faculty members. Furthermore, the institutions also may have to deal with negative media exposure, student protests (if the teacher is popular), charges of bias, and faculty factions (Leap 1993).

For administrators, there can be personal consequences. They face the possibility of being named codefendants in employment-discrimination cases. The department chair is particularly vulnerable as he or she may become the primary defendant if the decision at the department level is negative (LaNoue and Lee 1987). Chairs and other administrators also may have difficulty in getting their institutions to assist them financially in defending the lawsuit, and some administrators receive little moral support (LaNoue and Lee 1987).

The faculty member also suffers consequences. In addition to feeling hurt, a negative tenure decision may result in job loss. Since a negative decision typically is viewed by the academic community as a reflection of the individual's competence, the faculty member often has difficulty obtaining employment elsewhere*. Also, the faculty member may have his or her performance publicly exposed to criticism during the litigation. Since no one is perfect in all three categories—teaching, service, and scholarship—the faculty member may doubt his or her own abilities and the reasons for filing the lawsuit. Furthermore, the financial and political resources needed for these lengthy litigations also imposes a heavy burden on the faculty member (LaNoue and Lee 1987).

In their discussion of *Lieberman vs. Gant* (1979), *Scott vs. University of Delaware* (1978), and other cases, LaNoue and Lee excellently illustrated the impact of employment-discrimination litigation on everyone involved. *Lieberman*, a gender-discrimination case against the University of Connecticut, was long and complex, producing a transcript of nearly 10,000 pages and almost 400 exhibits and consuming 52 days of court time (the trial lasted more than two years). The 18 defendants, numerous legal claims, large number of witnesses, and the protracted illness of Lieberman's attorney produced an extremely lengthy litigation that required substantial human and financial resources from Lieberman and the University of Connecticut. Lieberman's personal consequences were severe. She not only lost the case but was financially ruined, forced to file bankruptcy to avoid legal-fee claims, lost her health and profession, and could have lost her marriage.

The impact on the faculty member in *Scott*, a race-discrimination case, also was great. This case challenged the Ph.D. requirement and the decentralized decision-making process as having a discriminatory impact upon African-American faculty members. The personal toll on Scott was extremely severe. Not only did he lose his case against the University of Delaware, but he died of a heart attack two days before his attorney argued his appeal. LaNoue and Lee

---

*This could have been one of the reasons for the Supreme Court decision in *Board of Regents vs. Roth* (1972). Roth, or more accurately his attorney, failed to show the likely effect of a negative employment decision on his professional reputation. Had this been proved, Roth would have implicated a "liberty interest," which entitled him to due process protection.

indicated that Scott's loss at the trial level, the necessity of leaving the university, his difficulty in obtaining employment in a related field, and the loss of his second position after one year because of layoffs probably combined to produce his fatal heart attack, especially since he had a history of heart disease.

The Legal Basis for Employment-Discrimination Lawsuits

Faculty members are protected from illegal discrimination by a number of state and federal laws. Federal law has assumed the greatest importance in discrimination cases (Kaplin and Lee 1995). There are nine major federal employment-discrimination laws and one major executive order, applicable to colleges and universities, each with its own comprehensive set of regulations and guidelines and which provide more protection than the Constitution and many state laws (Kaplin and Lee 1995).

Race discrimination in promotion, tenure, and reappointment is covered by Title VII of the Civil Rights Act of 1964 and Section 1981 of the Civil Rights Act of 1866. Gender discrimination is covered by Title VII and Title IX of the Education Amendments of 1972. Age discrimination is covered, in part, by the Age Discrimination in Employment Act of 1967. Discrimination against people with disabilities is covered by the Americans with Disabilities Act of 1990 and the Rehabilitation Act of 1973. Discrimination on the basis of religion is covered by Title VII. Discrimination on the basis of national origin is covered by Title VII. Discrimination based upon national origin is covered by Title VII (Kaplin and Lee 1995; LaNoue and Lee 1987).

Constitutional considerations

Faculty members at public institutions may be protected from employment discrimination by the due process and equal-protection clauses of the 14th Amendment. These lawsuits, however, rarely are successful since the Supreme Court ruled in *Washington vs. Davis* (1976) that employees must prove intentional discrimination to prevail on constitutional grounds. Proving intentional discrimination is extremely difficult given the confidential nature of the promotion and tenure process. Under federal civil-rights laws, employees may prove discrimination by showing that institutional policies have a negative and "disproportionate impact" on their particular class of employees (African-Americans or women, for example). Disproportionate impact is not a sufficient ground for proving discrimination under the Constitution.

The Constitution plays a small role in employment-discrimination cases. This is partly the result of a strict standard of proof. But the federal statutes have extended constitutional protection against employment discrimination. Furthermore, the 14th Amendment case does not give institutions the kind of guidance provided by detailed rules and regulations of federal law, and faculty members do not have the broad range of remedies (Kaplin 1985). Furthermore, constitutional protection only applies to faculty members at public institutions; faculty members at private colleges and universities have no recourse under the Constitution even if they are able to prove intentional discrimination.

The Constitution, however, assumes more importance in areas not covered by the federal civil-rights laws (Kaplin and Lee 1995). For example, discrimination against people younger than 40 years, or homosexuals, is not covered by the federal civil-rights laws (Kaplin and Lee 1995). If there are no local or state laws prohibiting these types of discrimination, the Constitution may be the only recourse for individuals so victimized by public institutions. In these situations, however, the alleged victims of discrimination will have to prove that the discrimination was intentional.

Title VII of the Civil Rights Act of 1964
Title VII of the Civil Rights Act of 1964 (42 U.S.C. § 2000e) is the most important legislation in employment discrimination and warrants the most extensive discussion in this report. Title VII is the most frequently used legislation in employment-discrimination cases (Hendrickson and Lee 1983; Kaplin and Lee 1995; Lee 1995). Congress was concerned with discrimination in higher education (especially that of women) when it amended Title VII to include private and public institutions (LaNoue and Lee 1987). Title VII concepts also parallel those under other federal civil-rights laws (Kaplin 1985).

Title VII makes it illegal for an institution to discriminate against faculty members on the basis of their race, gender, national origin, or religion, unless it is a necessary and "bona fide occupational qualification" (Kaplin and Lee 1995,

p. 199). This exception forms the legal basis for the practice of religious institutions of hiring faculty members of particular religious denominations.

To bring an action (sue) under Title VII, faculty members must establish a *prima facie*, or "on its face," claim; this means there is enough evidence to convince a court that discrimination may have occurred. A prima facie showing involves four steps. First, the faculty member must show that he or she was a member of the protected class Title VII covers. This is not difficult since anyone can be the victim of race, gender, religious, or national-origin discrimination. Second, the faculty member must show that he or she sought, and had the appropriate qualifications for, reappointment, promotion, and tenure — that he or she had the same qualifications as other successful candidates. Since these decisions are based on vague and subjective criteria, faculty members can show discrimination by proving that their qualifications compared favorably with other successful candidates in the department or that they received a favorable recommendation by the peer-review committees or external evaluators (Leap 1993). Third, the faculty member must show that he or she was not reappointed, promoted, or tenured. Finally, the faculty member must prove that the institution reappointed, promoted, or tenured, around the same time, other faculty members possessing similar qualifications.

In establishing a prima facie claim, faculty members will use evidence indicating that they compared favorably with others who were reappointed, promotion, or tenured. The criteria used in such comparisons include similarities in quantity and quality of publications; teaching abilities; and administrative responsibilities and committee work. The comparative data, however, must be so compelling as to lead a court to believe that discrimination has occurred rather than an honest difference of opinion among professionals qualified to make such judgments (Leap 1993).

Once the faculty member has established a prima facie claim, the institution must articulate some "legitimate business reason" for denying reappointment, promotion, or tenure. Usually, the institution attempts to show institutional financial problems, the elimination or scaling down of an academic program, tenure density, that the faculty member did not meet the appropriate criteria (teaching, service, or scholarship), or that the faculty member was incompatible with the department personally (he or she does not work well with others) or in terms of his or her research or teaching specialty (Hendrickson and Lee 1983; LaNoue and Lee 1987; Leap 1993).

The faculty member then has the burden of proving that the "legitimate business reason" articulated by the college was actually a pretext and that the actual motivation for the decision was discriminatory. Faculty members can show pretext by attacking the institution's motive and substantiating others or by showing statistical or comparative evidence that indicates that discrimination was the motivating factor in the decision (Hendrickson 1991). If the faculty member can demonstrate to a court that the stated reasons for the negative decision were not the actual reasons, then the court may infer that the institution illegally discriminated against the faculty member (Leap 1993).

On the other hand, if the institution can show that its faculty and administrators have used the stated criteria, followed their procedures, documented their reasons, and treated similar faculty members in the same way that the suing faculty member was treated, then it generally prevails in Title VII cases (LaNoue and Lee 1987). In *Bina vs. Providence College* (1994), a professor of Iranian descent sued the college alleging that the college was motivated by ethnic discrimination when it denied him a tenured teaching position. The court was persuaded that Bina was not discriminated against because the committee minutes clearly reflected objective appraisals of his qualifications.

Title VII claims first must be filed by the faculty member with the Equal Employment Opportunity Commission, or EEOC, within 180 days after the alleged discrimination has occurred. In states that have an approved civil-rights agency, the faculty members may have up to 300 days to file a Title VII complaint (Leap 1993). For reappointment, promotion, and tenure decisions, this means that the claims must be filed very shortly after the faculty member is notified of the negative decision, even if the institution provides him or her with a terminal year and an internal grievance proceeding (Kaplin 1985). These time limitations apply to each act of alleged discrimination.

The continuing violation doctrine, however, allows the faculty member to have an entire pattern of discrimination heard, even when the time limit for certain acts has expired. For example, in *Sunshine vs. Long Island University* (1994), a court held that a faculty member's pre-1992 claims were evidence of a continuing practice of discrimination against female faculty members. For six years Sunshine had been denied tenure by the academic vice president despite being recommended for tenure by the department, the dean, and the tenure committees.

Faculty members also must exhaust their administrative remedies, including filing a claim with the EEOC, before initiating a Title VII action in court. In *Moche vs. City University of New York* (1992), the court dismissed a gender-discrimination case because Moche had not filed a complaint with the EEOC or a qualified state agency nor did she obtain a "right to sue" letter from the EEOC. The EEOC issues "right to sue" letters allowing complainants to seek immediate legal recourse in court rather than waiting for the EEOC to complete its investigation.

Title VII also requires that the faculty members mitigate their damages. Faculty members may be required to seek and obtain other comparable employment to recover monetary damages. In *Ford vs. Nicks* (1989), for example, the court determined that Middle Tennessee State University discriminated against Ford, a female faculty member in its education and library science department, on the basis of gender. Ford was offered a position at a technical college 70 miles away, which she turned down because the commute was too far, and she did not actively seek an academic position after that. The court held that Title VII required that the faculty member look for and accept employment substantially equivalent to the job she lost. The court held that since she and her husband had looked nationally for positions and the technical college was close enough for the couple to have moved halfway between two cities to accommodate each other's work, monetary damages under Title VII stopped accruing as of the date on which she would have begun work at the technical college.

Categories of Title VII claims

Title VII claims fall into two major categories: disparate treatment and disparate impact. Faculty members allege disparate treatment when race, gender, or some other illegal motive affected the negative decision; disparate impact cases usually allege that reappointment, promotion, and tenure policies, practices, or criteria have an unfair, discriminatory impact on a certain class of people (Leap 1993; Kaplin 1985).

Disparate treatment. The elements of a disparate-treatment claim were outlined by the Supreme Court in *McDonnell Douglas Corp. vs. Green* (1973). Disparate-treatment cases require proof that the discrimination was intentional. Because intentional discrimination is difficult to prove, most faculty members who file such lawsuits rarely succeed. A court will not necessarily find that discrimination has occurred simply because a college or university failed to make "careful, well-reasoned personnel decisions or failed to follow prescribed procedures" (Leap 1993, p. 111). Women and faculty of color nevertheless have prevailed in these cases when they have been able to prove that they were held to higher standards of performance than white males or that they did not receive appropriate career counseling and timely evaluation appraisals, while others did. In some rare cases faculty members are able to prove directly that they were denied reappointment, promotion, and tenure because of collegial or administrator gender or racial discrimination.

The difficulty in Title VII cases is not in establishing a prima facie claim but in proving that the institution's stated reasons were a pretext for discrimination. In *Jackson vs. Harvard University* (1990), a female faculty member at Harvard University's Graduate School of Business Administration twice was rejected for tenure. During the initial proceedings, Jackson requested that an individual on her subcommittee be removed for having a bias against women. Her request was denied, but the subcommittee voted in her favor, with the individual she claimed was biased voting for her but expressing reservations about her work. Since the vote at the faculty meeting was split, her appointment was extended for three years. During the second proceedings, a slim majority of the faculty voted in her favor, but the dean denied her tenure. Jackson alleged that the dean (in referring to affirmative action) told her that if the government or the public wanted women faculty at the business school, they would have to impose quotas because Harvard would not actually promote women. The court held that although Jackson made a prima facie claim of discrimination, Harvard articulated a nondiscriminatory reason (deficient scholarship), and Jackson did not prove that the reason was pretextual. The court was persuaded that the dean in fact supported affirmative action and that the allegedly biased person actually voted in her favor.

A court reached a different conclusion in *Korbin vs. University of Minnesota* (1994). An appeals court found that the institution's stated reasons for not reappointing a female faculty member in the comparative literature department were a pretext for discrimination. In 1988 the department hired Korbin as a lecturer after her position at another program was eliminated. Shortly after, the department approved two new positions, a senior and a junior position. Korbin applied for the junior position and was one of the 15 finalists, but the committee chose another candidate. When the senior position could not be filled, the department received permission to hire another junior faculty member. The department chose a male candidate to fill the position, and Korbin then initiated a gender-discrimination suit.

The district court held in favor of the university. The appeals court overturned the decision, determining that the university's reasons were pretextual. This court found that the university's reasons changed over time. First it informed Korbin that the male candidate was hired because of his experience in critical theory and psychoanalysis, then claimed that he was more qualified than Korbin because her background in critical theory was too focused on psychoanalysis. The university claimed that Korbin's expertise in psychoanalysis was not one of the areas it was attempting to fill, yet the male candidate was assigned to the courses in psychoanalysis and literature — courses Korbin had developed. So clearly the university vacillated in its reasoning.

When women or faculty of color are treated differently, courts become suspicious. In *Kunda vs. Muhlenberg College* (1978), the court determined that a female faculty member in the physical-education department was discriminated against on the basis on her gender. Kunda was denied promotion and tenure and sued the college alleging that she was treated differently than the males in her department. The college contended that she was not promoted and tenured because she did not have a master's degree. But Kunda was able to show that unlike the males in her depart-

When women or faculty of color are treated differently, courts become suspicious.

ment she was never counseled that a master's degree was essential for tenure. The Kunda case is important for a number of reasons, primarily because of the remedies the court granted*. This case also recognized the importance of peer review in promotion and tenure decisions — the faculty-review committees had agreed that Kunda was qualified (LaNoue and Lee 1987). Courts, and especially juries, may be convinced that discrimination has occurred when the faculty member receives peer support at the departmental level and by external reviewers (Lee 1995). *Kunda* also made it clear that although courts will defer to the expert judgments of college officials, institutions of higher education are not insulated from Title VII liability (Kaplin 1985).

Women or faculty of color who can prove that they were held to a higher standard than white males are likely to prevail. Sometimes, this is obvious. In *Gutzwiller vs. Fenik* (1988), a female faculty member in the University of Cincinnati's classics department was denied promotion and tenure. At the time that Gutzwiller was hired, there were 12 faculty members in the department, and the only woman in the department had been denied tenure. The department head, Fenik, had informed Gutzwiller that her book based upon her dissertation was not enough and that she should publish another book independent of her dissertation. No male member of the department needed to publish a second book.

Gutzwiller asked the new department head for a leave in order to publish her book, but her request was denied. Her request for a reduced load (to which she was entitled after four years of service) was not granted until just before she was to apply for promotion and tenure, which prevented any possibility of publishing her book. The court determined that Gutzwiller had been discriminated against because of gender. It based this decision upon several findings: No male member of the department was required to publish a second book; she met or exceeded the number of publications of every tenured member except the committee chair; the committee chair treated her unequally in the selection of outside evaluators (only two of the reviewers that she selected were chosen, while men usually had all five of

---

*The court granted Kunda "conditional tenure"; in other words, she would attain tenure when she obtained her master's degree.

their selections chosen); the chair of the tenure committees consistently provided negative interpretations to generally favorable evaluations of her scholarship; and the department chair consistently had opposed her, affirmative action, and women in tenured positions.

The *Gutzwiller* case not only provides an example of obvious discrimination but also is an example of when individual administrators can be found guilty of violating a faculty member's civil rights. The court stated that the department and committee chairs acted "recklessly" and with "callous disregard" for Gutzwiller's rights when they influenced the decision to deny her tenure; they therefore could be held liable for punitive damages under Section 1983, which allows faculty members to sue public-school officials who have violated their constitutional rights.

In *Brown vs. Trustees of Boston University* (1989), an appeals court also found that the institution's stated reasons for denying promotion and tenure to a female faculty member in the College of Liberal Arts were pretextual, and that a woman was held to a higher standard than males in her department. Brown's application for promotion and tenure listed a book on Jane Austen based upon her dissertation (which was published by Harvard University Press and nominated for an award), three book reviews, and a work in progress about Oscar Wilde (for which she received a $16,000 Mellon grant). The department committee voted unanimously in favor of promotion and tenure, and the dean agreed after expressing reservations about her scholarship. The dean, however, suggested that a historian be solicited to review her work and that she be granted a three-year extension to finish her work on Wilde (this extension was permitted under the collective-bargaining agreement provided that the tenure committees and the candidate all agree).

The universitywide committee voted 9-2 to grant Brown promotion and tenure. The assistant provost, the provost, and the president, expressing concern about the quality of her book, recommended the three-year extension. All of the committees and Brown rejected the extension. An ad hoc committee voted 2-1 in favor of promotion and tenure. The provost, however, recommended against tenure because the committee vote was not an unqualified endorsement. The president agreed. Brown's Title VII lawsuit claimed that she had been subjected to a higher standard than males in the department because no external historian was sought for them; other males had been granted tenure with smaller quantities of published works; the males also had books based upon their dissertations; no male candidate in the English department had a second published book; some of the males granted tenure had not published any book; and their tenure reviews were not as strong as hers. The trial court held in Brown's favor and ordered that she be reinstated and tenured. The appeals court agreed and held that a faculty member's right to be free from discrimination prevents the university's tenure process from being insulated from judicial review. The appeals court indicated that inference of discrimination can be made by showing that the university's stated reasons for denying promotion or tenure were obviously weak or implausible or that the tenure standards were unequally applied.

The actions of key administrators in these types of cases also is informative. In *Brown*, the court permitted the faculty member to include evidence of administrator bias. For example, Brown introduced comments by the president referring to her department as a "damn matriarchy" despite the small proportion of women in the department. In *Sunshine vs. Long Island University* (1994), a female faculty member in the political-science department was denied tenure from 1987 to 1992 by the academic vice president after her department, the dean, and the Faculty Personnel Committee all endorsed her application. Sunshine had been informed in 1985 and 1986 that she would be granted tenure once she obtained her Ph.D., which she did; then the academic vice president informed her that she would not be tenured until she had additional publications, and when she published more articles he still rejected her application. In 1992, 12 professors — five males and seven females — were recommended for tenure by their departments and the faculty. All of the males except a Hispanic were granted tenure, and initially none of the women were. After a faculty protest, one of the females was tenured. Two of the women involved in the protest, including Sunshine, were released.

During a meeting of the faculty, the academic vice president allegedly made knowingly false and defamatory statements about Sunshine's qualifications as a scholar. Sunshine's lawsuit alleged that she had been the victim of gender discrimination and that she was released in retaliation for her complaints about the treatment of women faculty. The court held that she had sufficient evidence to sustain an action for illegal discrimination because of the department's weak record of granting tenure to women, and males had been granted tenure despite fewer publications than Sunshine. Sunshine also demonstrated enough evidence to sustain a retaliation claim. She was released after she filed an internal grievance and was involved in the faculty protest. The academic vice president's allegedly defamatory remarks also helped to support the retaliation claim.

These examples all involve gender discrimination. Race-discrimination claims are much more difficult to show. In *Scott vs. University of Delaware* (1978), an African-American faculty member in the sociology department sued the university alleging race discrimination when he was not reappointed for a second three-year term. The university contended that his teaching and scholarship were inadequate. The thrust of Scott's argument regarding the disparate-treatment claim was that white faculty members generally were renewed for additional periods and thus afforded greater opportunity to qualify for tenure. The court rejected his claim and determined that the decision of his professional colleagues was based upon their belief that Scott was not interested in pursuing the kind of scholarship, research, and writing they believed important and that his teaching was not effective — all legitimate reasons for not reappointing him.

Courts will find race discrimination in more obvious situations. In *Clark vs. Claremont University Center* (1992), the appeals court found that the university discriminated against an African-American male faculty member in its education department. Clark's departmental review was positive, but the two senior members (the former and current department chairmen who guided Clark through the tenure process) voted against him. The university tenure committee voted against tenure by a 4-1 vote. Clark appealed to the president, who investigated his racial-discrimination allegations and found that at a departmental meeting, a faculty member who voted against Clark had said, "Us white folks have rights, too."

The president, however, affirmed the committee's decision because of what he claimed was Clark's insufficient publication record and negative student evaluations. The university appealed the trial court's decision in favor of Clark, and the appeals court upheld the verdict. Although each step of the review process purportedly resulted in a different review of Clark's application, the court strongly believed that the department's review was discriminatory and it affected the subsequent decisions — especially since negative evaluations had to be submitted to the subsequent reviewers. The court also found that the chairperson misled Clark concerning publication requirements and gave him a discriminatory review; the faculty member making the "racial" remark wrote a negative letter to the tenure committee; another faculty member's mention of Clark's race in a tenure committee meeting was a subterfuge for discrimination (the faculty member claimed he was reminding the tenure committee of its affirmative-action obligation); Claremont had never granted tenure to a person of color; external scholars had commented on the excellence of Clark's work and the groundbreaking nature of Clark's book; white professors were tenured with less substantial publishing records; and Claremont had changed its unwritten publication standards to justify its denial of tenure to Clark. The court also believed that the president's review ignored substantial evidence of discrimination and was merely a rubber stamp of the tenure committee's decision.

Clark notwithstanding, racial-discrimination claims are extremely difficult to prove unless the faculty member is white and the institution is historically black. For example, in *Craig vs. Alabama State University* (1978), the court determined that the university had engaged in a pattern of discrimination against white professors. And in *Whiting vs. Jackson State University* (1980), the court determined that a white professor's discharge was motivated by his race. The claims by historically black institutions that African-American faculty members provide better role models than white professors have not been accepted by courts when the institutions use race-conscious employment decisions (Kaplin and Lee 1995). Why lawsuits by white professors against historically black institutions are more likely to succeed than lawsuits by faculty of color against predominantly white institutions is a phenomenon that deserves more research.

Disparate impact. Disparate-impact claims are less common in higher education (Kaplin and Lee 1995). The elements of a disparate-impact claim were outlined by the Supreme Court in *Griggs vs. Duke Power Co.* (1971), which held that Title VII prohibits those practices that exclude or otherwise discriminate against faculty members on the basis of race, sex, religion, or national origin and that are unrelated to job performance or not justified by business necessity. Later, the Supreme Court ruled that a challenged practice need not be "essential" or "indispensable" to an employer's interest for the practice to pass judicial scrutiny. The Civil Rights Act of 1991 reversed this later Supreme Court ruling and others which had limited the rights of persons filing civil-rights lawsuits. Now, institutions must show that the practice is job-related and necessary.

The subjective nature of the promotion and tenure process makes it difficult for faculty members to prove discrimination. But the Supreme Court has permitted challenges to subjective criteria. In *Watson vs. Fort Worth Bank & Trust* (1988), the Supreme Court determined that employees can attack subjective decision-making practices under the disparate-impact theory. This is important because reappointment, promotion, and tenure decisions often are based upon subjective performance standards (Kaplin and Lee 1995).

In disparate-impact cases, faculty members often rely upon statistics to show that a particular criterion has a nontrivial disparity on their class of plaintiffs (statistics showing that the Ph.D. requirements negatively impact the number of faculty of color who may attain tenure, for example). Institutions often argue in these cases that this evidence is unreliable. The use of statistics in disparate-impact cases is important, however, because it provides courts with indirect evidence of discrimination and allows them to avoid dealing with the merits of a negative decision (Leap 1995).

Once the faculty member establishes the nontrivial disparity, the institution must show there is a "business necessity" for the challenged criteria (Swan 1990, p. 555). In *Griggs* (1971), the Supreme Court held that the employer may show that a criterion having a disparate impact on a particular class of people may be valid if there is a business necessity. The criterion would be illegal if it is unrelated to job performance. The faculty member then must show that the institution's stated reasons were a pretext for illegal discrimination. It is at this stage in disparate-treatment and -impact cases that faculty members introduce comparative evidence (Leap 1993). As noted, most faculty members have lost their cases. A study published nine years ago indicated that only one in five faculty members win their cases* (LaNoue and Lee 1987).

Courts occasionally have asked colleges and universities to show that their required qualifications for promotion and tenure are job-related if the qualifications exclude a disproportionate number of women and persons of color (Lee 1985). In *Scott vs. Delaware* (1978), Scott filed both disparate-treatment and -impact claims. His disparate-impact claim involved a class-action suit alleging that the university's doctoral-degree criterion had a discriminatory impact on African-American faculty members and was not justified by the legitimate needs of the university, and that the decentralized and subjective decision-making process had the overall effect of putting African-American candidates at a disadvantage.

Although the court acknowledged that the Ph.D. requirement had a disproportionate impact on African-Americans, the court held that it was justified by the legitimate interest of the university in hiring and advancing faculty members who are likely to be successful in adding knowledge to their disciplines and effective in the teaching of graduate students. The court held that Scott failed to suggest an alternative which would serve the interests of the university and have a less adverse effect on African-Americans, nor did Scott prove evidence that the decentralized and subjective nature of the process discriminated against African-Americans. The court believed that the lack of a critical mass of African-American faculty had more to do with self-selection than discrimination, noting that all of the African-Americans on staff with a doctorate and three or more years of experience were tenured or near tenure. And no other faculty member, African-American or white, had ever been denied a mid-term contract renewal or ever alleged racial discrimination.

The *Scott* case is important because it was the most serious attack on the Ph.D., the "union card for admission to the

---

*These numbers do not take into consideration settlements, or cases that were never litigated. There are no recent studies indicating whether this still is true today.

academic profession," and the requirement of which does have a statistically negative impact on the number of African-Americans and other underrepresented groups in the faculty ranks (LaNoue and Lee 1987, p. 116). Scott also had asked that one of three new faculty hires at all levels of the university be African-American until they made up 12.5 percent of the total faculty. The case, therefore, had the potential to bring compulsory affirmative-action requirements to research universities.

Prevailing under a disparate-impact claim is extremely difficult. In *J. Carpenter vs. Board of Regents, University of Wisconsin* (1984), an African-American male faculty member in the Afro-American studies department at the university's Milwaukee campus sued under the disparate-treatment and -impact theories. Because the department was new, Carpenter was required to perform more responsibilities, including curriculum and course development, and he served as chairman for the academic year 1975-76. Carpenter also performed heavy counseling and advising for African-American students at the predominantly white campus, and he performed service in the community. These activities — some necessary because of the absence of senior faculty at the new department and others important because of the special needs of African-American students and his volunteer work — curtailed his ability to spend time on his scholarship.

Carpenter requested that two years of prior service be eliminated from the tenure clock so that he could have more time to spend on his research, but this request was denied purportedly because it was not permitted by the procedures. Carpenter submitted his materials, and the department and college committees recommended tenure. The dean did not support tenure because of Carpenter's deficiency in scholarship and research. As a result, tenure was denied and Carpenter appealed to the top of the university system, to the state's Equal Rights Division, the EEOC, and the Office of Civil Rights of the Labor Department — most concluding that race was a factor in the tenure decision.

Carpenter sued, alleging the disparate-treatment and -impact theories of race discrimination, but the district court held that Carpenter was not discriminated against under either theory. He appealed the disparate-impact holding. The appeals court did not find that African-Americans were disproportionately denied tenure. Carpenter tried to show with nonstatistical, qualitative evidence that the tenure standards had a disparate impact on African-Americans because of the many additional burdens in teaching and service borne by African-American junior faculty. Carpenter also alleged that the application of the seven-year rule created a disparate impact on African-American faculty given the pressures they faced. The court rejected all of his claims. Disparate-impact claims, therefore, are very difficult to prove.

Remedies under Title VII
The Civil Rights Act of 1991 increased the potential financial liability that institutions may face if found guilty of discrimination. Faculty members who are victims of illegal discrimination may receive compensation for lost wages, emotional pain, suffering, inconvenience, mental anguish, loss of employment, and other nonpecuniary losses. Faculty members also may receive compensation for loss of a future salary; this remedy may be recovered in lieu of reinstatement if the faculty member is likely to face antagonism and retaliation. Faculty members also may recover attorney's fees, adjustment of benefits, and other cash awards. Furthermore, the institution also may have to pay punitive damages if it is found to have intentionally discriminated; the cap on this amount, however, is $300,000 (Leap 1993). Title VII also limits the recovery of back pay for a period of two years (Hendrickson and Lee 1983). As mentioned previously, faculty members are required to mitigate their damages before they can recover fully under Title VII.

The most controversial awards for discrimination involve reinstatement, promotion, and tenure. Courts rarely award these remedies, stating that they are not qualified to determine whether faculty members would have attained them but for the discrimination. When the discrimination is clearly established, courts have determined that Title VII requires that the faculty member be made whole, which means, in certain cases, a requirement that the faculty member be reinstated, promoted, or tenured. In *Brown vs. Boston University* (1989), the appeals courts upheld the jury's award of $200,000 for breach of contract, the trial judge's award of damages for emotional distress, and reinstatement to the position of associate professor with tenure.

The *Kunda vs. Muhlenberg College* (1978) case is mainly

known for its unusual remedy. Kunda was awarded reinstatement, back pay, promotion to associate professor, and the opportunity to complete her master's degree within two years, after which she would receive tenure. This case is, to date, the only example of a judicial award of "conditional tenure" (LaNoue and Lee 1987).

Despite *Kunda, Brown,* and other such cases, courts are still reluctant to mandate tenure. Courts are more likely to award loss of future salary and other monetary damages in lieu of tenure. In *Ford vs. Nicks* (1989), the appeals court upheld the faculty member's reinstatement but determined that the district court abused its discretion in mandating tenure, where the university's tenure system specifically required approval by the board of trustees.

The awards in lieu of tenure, however, can be substantial. In *Clark vs. Claremont University Center* (1992), Clark was awarded $1 million in compensatory damages, $16,327 in punitive damages, and attorney's fees of $419,833.13. The appeals court upheld this award. In *Rajender vs. University of Minnesota* (1983), the final consent decree in this sex-discrimination litigation resulted in an award for the faculty member of $100,000, a quota for the hiring of women, and a requirement that three special "masters" be appointed to resolve all past or future sex-discrimination grievances against the university (Leap 1993, p. 162).

Section 1981 and Section 1983

Section 1981 of the Civil Rights Act of 1866 prohibits discrimination on the basis of race or national origin and has been used by people of color and people who are not U.S. citizens to challenge negative employment decisions (Hendrickson and Lee 1983). Unlike Title VII, Section 1981 does not impose any limit on compensatory or punitive damages (Leap 1993). The standard of proof, however, is the same as with the 14th Amendment: To prevail under Section 1981 the faculty member must show that the institution intentionally discriminated against his or her race or citizenship (Kaplin).

Section 1983 of the Civil Rights Act of 1871 prohibits any person acting "under color" of any state or local law from depriving any individual of his or her constitutional and legal rights. Section 1983 also requires proof of intentional discrimination, and many public officials are afforded immunity unless the actions were blatantly and intentionally illegal — a very difficult standard to overcome. Since discrimination is usually well-hidden, it is extremely difficult to prevail under these laws. As a result, few cases are brought under these civil-rights statutes. To prevail under sections 1981 or 1983, the discrimination must be so indiscreet or the discriminatory actions somehow must be recorded — highly unlikely situations (LaNoue and Lee 1987).

Title IX of the Education Amendments of 1972
Title IX of the Education Amendments of 1972 prohibits gender-based discrimination in educational institutions receiving federal financial aid, and it is administered by the Office of Civil Rights of the Education Department. The regulations are similar to those promulgated by the EEOC (Kaplin 1985). The standards for proving discrimination under Title IX are similar to those of Title VII; faculty members may prove disparate treatment or impact. If alleging disparate treatment, faculty members must prove intentional discrimination (Kaplin and Lee 1995).

Most of the litigation involving Title IX has dealt with the scope of coverage of the law; few cases have addressed specific discriminatory actions. Nevertheless, Title IX is an important statute for faculty members who may be victimized by gender discrimination for a number of reasons. First, Title IX allows faculty members direct access to a court, while Title VII requires them to pursue administrative remedies through the EEOC before initiating a lawsuit (Hendrickson 1991). Second, Title IX permits faculty members to receive uncapped compensatory and punitive damages, while Title VII limits the amount of damages one may recover. Finally, Title IX borrows the statute of limitations from state law, while Title VII has a very short time frame in which claims must be filed (Kaplin and Lee 1995). The use of Title IX for suits based on gender discrimination, therefore, is likely to increase.

Age Discrimination
The Age Discrimination in Employment Act of 1967, or ADEA, prohibits age discrimination against people who are at least 40 years old. As of Jan. 1, 1994, no faculty member may be forced to retire at any age, although voluntary retirement plans are valid (Leap 1993). The ADEA standards are

similar to those of Title VII. The faculty member must offer a prima facie showing of age discrimination, at which point the college must show that age is a "bona fide occupational qualification necessary to the normal operation of the particular business" or that the decision was not based upon age (Kaplin 1985, pp. 141-2).

The standards for prevailing under the ADEA are just as stringent as those under Title VII. In *Fisher vs. Asheville-Buncombe Technical College* (1993), a faculty member of electrical engineering technology who had served the college for 20 years on a series of one-year contracts was not reappointed. The department had instituted a new curriculum, deemphasizing some existing teaching concepts and adding other concepts. Fisher had trouble with the new responsibilities and continued teaching the outmoded concepts, and when confronted on one occasion challenged the department head to a fistfight in front of students. He was transferred out of the department and later informed that he would not be rehired. He was 61 years old, and the college filled his position with someone who was 36 years old.

Fisher filed a suit alleging age discrimination under the ADEA, introducing as evidence the department head's comments that he needed "new blood" because Fisher was "outdated," "too old," "behind the times," and the like. The court determined that the department head's comments did not prove that he intended to fire Fisher and replace him with a younger person. Such statements are indicative of bias, but they are unlawful only if acted upon. The court held that it is not unlawful to require older employees to remain current in their jobs and to fire them if they fail to do so. The ADEA does not prohibit a younger person from replacing an older one nor does it require that faculty members be released only for good reasons. It only requires that the faculty members not be discharged because of their age.

In another example illustrating the difficulty of prevailing under the ADEA, Joan Goodship was denied tenure in the University of Richmond's education department purportedly because of the quality of her research and scholarship (*Goodship vs. University of Richmond* 1994). When she was hired, her future supervisor noted on her file, "Goodship will be 61 at tenure time = morally obligated to tenure — do we want this?" Goodship received positive performance reviews from 1988 through 1992 but was cautioned in 1990

The court held that it is not unlawful to require older employees to remain current in their jobs and to fire them if they fail to do so.

by the dean of faculty that she needed to get her research published. She had two articles published, but she received many negative comments regarding the quality of her scholarship and research. Three of her department peers recommended tenure, and one did not. The tenure committee unanimously recommended against tenure, as did the dean, provost, and president.

During the time of Goodship's review, the university was fostering an early-retirement program which Goodship contended was evidence that the university promoted a "youth culture," and she submitted affidavits regarding negative comments made, and pressures exerted, against older faculty. The court held that she did not satisfy the fourth element of a prima facie claim. She was a member of a protected group; she was denied tenure; she was performing in a satisfactory manner; but she did not prove that the university replaced her with a younger person. The court, however, indicated that even if she had established a prima facie claim, the university successfully showed that the tenure denial was due to her deficient scholarship and research. The comments placed in her file were made when she was hired, and she did not indicate that she was ill-treated in the interim. The early-retirement program, without anything more, is not evidence of discrimination. The court indicated that such a plan actually gives older employees an option not available to younger ones.

Discrimination Based on Physical Disabilities
The Rehabilitation Act of 1973 (Section 504) and the Americans with Disabilities Act of 1990, or ADA, prohibit discrimination against qualified people with disabilities. A qualified person with a disability is one who, with reasonable accommodation, can perform the essential functions of the job. The acts also require that institutions make reasonable accommodations to known physical or mental disabilities unless this would impose an undue hardship (Kaplin 1985). The ADA expands the rights guaranteed by Section 504 and imposes more obligations on institutions (Hill 1992). Both laws are patterned after Title VII and Title IX.

More attention in higher education has been paid to cases involving students with disabilities. And although there are cases involving employees, cases involving faculty members with disabilities are rare (Leap 1993).

Nevertheless, the number of people with disabilities is increasing, and the higher-education community is becoming more aware of their needs and legal rights (Rothstein 1991). Colleges and universities should be prepared for this increase in disabled people. Rothstein recommends that institutions adopt policies clearly defining "disability" and describing what constitutes illegal discrimination in hiring, promotion, and retention (1991). In addition, people who coordinate services for the disabled and who ensure compliance with Section 504 and the ADA should be appointed. Furthermore, the higher-education community needs to be educated about the needs of people with disabilities, their rights, and how to make facilities and programs barrier-free.

Religion Discrimination
Title VII prohibits discrimination on the basis of religion. The bona fide occupational qualification, or BFOQ, exception, however, permits colleges to employ faculty members of a "particular religion" if the institution is "owned, supported, controlled, or managed by a particular religion or the institution's curriculum is directed toward a propagation of a particular religion" (Kaplin 1985, p. 138). In *Pime vs. Loyola University of Chicago* (1986), the university's policy of reserving certain tenure-track positions in its philosophy department for Jesuits was upheld as a BFOQ for its teaching philosophy (Kaplin and Lee 1990).

The primacy of the First Amendment over Title VII was illustrated in *E.E.O.C. vs. Catholic University of America* (1994). In this case, a nun who had been denied tenure in the canon law department brought a Title VII action against the university alleging gender discrimination. The court held that the First Amendment precluded the district court from deciding the employment-discrimination action. The canon law department had a special status within the university as one of three ecclesiastical departments. The Vatican retained ultimate authority over the department and approved all tenured faculty members. The Establishment clause of the First Amendment prohibits the government from entangling itself in an institution's religious affairs. As a result, the district court is precluded from deciding the Title VII case. According to the court, judicial evaluation of the quality of this nun's scholarship in the canon law department and prolonged monitoring and investigation by EEOC would have constituted excessive entanglement with religion.

Professor Y and Professor X Scenarios

Let us now consider the scenarios that began this section. Professor Y likely would base his disparate-treatment claim on Title VII's prohibition against race discrimination. If he can substantiate his claims, Professor Y likely would establish a prima facie claim: He is an African-American; he probably satisfies the paper qualifications (degree, experience, etc.); he was denied tenure; and other faculty members were tenured with similar or less qualifications. Private University, however, may be able to show a "legitimate business reason" for the denial. A court probably would not question the university's publications or research criteria or how they are applied; courts likely would consider the application of these criteria within the discretion of academic professionals.

And Private University's decision, based upon the claim that Professor Y is "hard to get along with," if proved with statements from students and colleagues, probably would be considered valid or at least negate the claims of bias. If Professor Y can establish, as the faculty member did in *Clark*, that the "racist" remarks impacted the decision against him (that is, that the department vote would have been stronger) and that the subsequent reviewers were motivated by discrimination or were influenced by the discriminatory decisions of the department committee, then he may be able to show that the university's reasons were pretextual. Furthermore, he may be able to introduce statistics and comparative data showing that no African-American has ever been tenured or that white faculty members have been tenured with less qualifications. If Professor Y should prevail, Title VII would permit the court to order the university to grant him tenure although a court is more likely to award him monetary damages.

Professor X also would be able to make a disparate-treatment claim under Title VII, but there is enough information indicating that she also may have a disparate-impact claim against Public University. Furthermore, she also may have disparate-treatment and -impact claims under Title IX and perhaps constitutional claims as well (because it is a public institution). To prevail on constitutional grounds, Professor X would have to prove intentional discrimination, which would be difficult. Professor X likely would establish a prima facie showing: She is female, with appropriate qualifications, who has been denied promotion, while men with similar or fewer qualifications were promoted.

The university can show a legitimate reason for the denial: namely, that Professor X did not have the necessary publications. She may be able to show that she was treated differently than the males in her department (that she was misled as to what she needed to do to be promoted). This is what happened in *Kunda*. Should Professor X prevail, the court may order the university to promote her; promotion to full professor may not be as drastic a remedy as tenure. The disparate-impact claim is based upon her arguments that a second book requirement disproportionately impacts women. But a second book requirement may be "legitimate," and courts are extremely reluctant to substitute their judgments of what is an appropriate qualification for an institution. Furthermore, Professor X may not be able to establish an alternative that would satisfy the institution's need to have qualified full professors and be less discriminatory toward women.

Summary

Employment-discrimination cases are increasing. Not only are women and faculty of color increasingly filing such lawsuits, but white males also increasingly are alleging race discrimination for negative reappointment, promotion, and tenure decisions. As a result, it is important for faculty and administrators to be familiar with employment-discrimination issues.

Although the U.S. Constitution and state laws prohibit discrimination, the bulk of the employment-discrimination litigation has involved a number of federal civil-rights laws, especially Title VII of the Civil Rights Act of 1964. Federal civil-rights laws impose a lighter burden of proof on faculty members alleging illegal discrimination than does the Constitution. These laws also provide better guidance for institutions for avoiding discrimination.

The best advice for avoiding these types of lawsuits is to treat everyone fairly and to judge faculty members on their merits. This advice is too simple, of course. Given the inherent subjectivity of the promotion and tenure process, what is considered fair or meritorious is difficult to determine and will vary from person to person. Furthermore, some policies or practices adversely affect women and faculty of color; these should be reviewed to ensure that they are necessary and that better alternatives do not exist to protect the individual rights of all faculty members while still ensuring a diverse and qualified faculty. Regardless of whether these reviews are made, colleges and universities should justify their reappointment, promotion, and tenure decisions with clear data and careful documentation (Hendrickson and Lee 1983).

AFFIRMATIVE ACTION, DIVERSITY, AND INDIVIDUAL RIGHTS

Consider this scenario:

Southern State University has implemented an affirmative-action plan in an effort to eliminate the effects of
its prior race and gender discrimination. University
officials believe that general societal discrimination has
led to low representation of faculty members who are
women or people of color. But more importantly for
the university, its own past discrimination has led to a
serious underrepresentation of women and people of
color in its faculty ranks, so the university has had a
difficult time attracting and retaining such faculty members. In addition to directing its various schools and
colleges to consider positively the gender, race, and
ethnic background of faculty candidates, the university
also rewards schools and colleges that can increase the
number of qualified tenured faculty members who are
women and people of color. Specifically, the university
uses money, space, and internal grants as incentives to
increase the diversity of its faculty. Furthermore, the
central administration has set aside a portion of its budget for tenured faculty lines for departments that want
to retain an "outstanding" traditionally underrepresented candidate but do not have the necessary resources.

What legal bases does Southern State University have to
justify its affirmative-action plan? Would this plan hold up in
court?

Few topics are as controversial in this society today as
affirmative action. Affirmative action has been referred to as
"a time bomb primed to detonate in the middle of the
American political marketplace" (Roberts 1995, p. 32).
Politicians are running campaigns threatening to eliminate
any programs promoting gender and racial preferences, and
this issue — or more accurately, the rhetoric over this issue
— may determine the outcome of important elections,
including that for the presidency of the United States.
Courts also increasingly are hearing cases challenging affirmative-action plans. This attack on affirmative action probably is due to a slow-growing economy, stagnant middle-class
incomes, and employer downsizing — all of which make
the decision of who gets hired, promoted, and fired much
more volatile.

Higher education has not been spared from this controversy (see Cahn 1993; *Chronicle of Higher Education*, April 28, 1995). The perception is strong that white faculty members are being discriminated against as a result of affirmative action. The reality, however, is that the percentage of women faculty and faculty of color lags far behind that of white males. The 1995 edition of the *Chronicle of Higher Education Almanac* lists the percentage of full-time female faculty members at 27.9 percent. African-Americans, Asians, Hispanics, and Native Americans made up, respectively 4.9, 5.3, 2.5, and 0.5 percent of all full-time faculty members. The old adage that "numbers can lie" does not seem to apply here. It is apparent to all that women and faculty of color are seriously underrepresented in the faculty ranks of American institutions of higher education.

Most affirmative-action plans favor women, African-Americans, Asian-Americans, Latinos, and Native Americans, but each group benefits differently at different institutions. For example, Mexican-Americans may benefit more than Asian-Americans at Western institutions than they might at Eastern institutions because there is a larger number of Asian-Americans at these institutions, or Asian-Americans are perceived as not needing preferential treatment (see Chan and Wang 1991). Opponents of any program that benefits any particular group contend that all racial and gender preferences should be made illegal. They argue that innocent people (often referring to white males) should not have to pay for the "sins" of others. Affirmative action in faculty employment is controversial because it potentially poses a conflict between two important American and higher education values: that all candidates deserve an equal opportunity to be hired, promoted, and tenured, and that hard work and merit — not race, gender, religion, or any other characteristic for which they have no control — should determine which candidates succeed.

In higher education, recent demographic and ethical trends have made the racial and gender diversity of the faculty an important goal. By increasing diversity, often accomplished through affirmative-action programs, colleges and universities sometimes have been accused of violating the individual rights of some faculty members. And although courts and legislatures often have been involved in these disputes, institutions of higher education must learn how to balance the need for diversity with the protection of individual rights without clear guidance from courts or legislatures.

While courts have upheld preferential treatment for people of color and women in some situations, they often have done so with reservations and conflicting guidance. Given the importance of this issue in higher education, faculty members and college administrators should have some sense of the legal implications of affirmative action. Readers should understand, however, that given the inconsistency of the courts, and the social and political climate in this country, any discussion of the legal implications of affirmative action must be tenuous at best.

Arguments For and Against Affirmative Action

Proponents of affirmative action have defined it as a "response to a history of discriminatory attitudes and actions against nonwhite people that prevented them from realizing opportunities that were available to whites, even when the nonwhites had equal or superior qualifications" (see Washington and Harvey 1989, p. 9). This definition takes into consideration the historical reality of discrimination in its definition. Opponents may see the issue more simply: They have defined affirmative action as "giving special treatment to some candidates on the basis of their membership in a target group" (see Markie 1993, p. 276). An institution's affirmative-action program will give some groups preferential treatment in reappointment, promotion, and tenure decisions, but the reasons for doing so are to eliminate the effects of the institution's own or societal discrimination.

Affirmative action has been justified as a step toward a more just society (Francis 1993) and has had wide support in academia (see "AAUP Re-Endorses Affirmative Action" 1995; Cahn 1993; Washington and Harvey 1989; West 1993). Affirmative action also has been criticized as leading to "reverse discrimination" and heavily opposed (see Markie 1993; Sowell 1990; Steele 1990). The opposition seems be growing today, and some colleges and universities are reconsidering their affirmative-action policies. For example, the regents of the University of California voted on July 20, 1995, to end affirmative action in admissions and hiring, apparently in response to political pressure (*Chronicle of Higher Education*, Aug. 4, 1995).

Proponents of affirmative action contend that the lack of

a diverse faculty undermines important institutional goals. Affirmative action which increases the hiring and promotion of a diverse faculty is important because these faculty members bring to the campus new perspectives based upon their experiences and backgrounds; they provide role models for students; they prepare students of color to assume leadership roles; they support scholarship dealing with race and gender issues; and they challenge the notion that women and faculty of color are not competent (Washington and Harvey 1989).

Students who are women and members of racial and ethnic minorities, whose numbers have increased at many colleges and universities, especially benefit from a diverse faculty. Some of these students have not encountered a person of color in a faculty position. Before these students move into leadership positions, it can be argued, they must encounter and interact with women and faculty of color in order to challenge the "myth about the intellectual and cultural inferiority of minority groups" (Washington and Harvey 1989, p. 3). To increase the number of women and faculty of color in academia, diverse role models and mentors are needed to encourage and support their entering the academic profession.

Women and faculty of color have made many gains in academia but still face discrimination. Although antidiscrimination laws are intended to protect them from illegal discrimination, these laws often are not enough to prevent it (see Washington and Harvey 1989; West 1993). The nature of the reappointment, promotion, and tenure process makes it exceptionally difficult to prove discrimination. And even if a faculty member is able to obtain enough financial, legal, and moral assistance to pursue a discrimination lawsuit, courts generally defer to the institution's expertise in these employment matters. Antidiscrimination law may be slow, costly, and piecemeal and thus inadequate to the challenge of ending discrimination (Clague 1987). Affirmative action, therefore, corrects for discriminatory practices in the promotion and tenure process because these practices usually are subtle and difficult to eradicate (Francis 1993).

Opponents of affirmative action contend that it is unethical because it involves doing an injustice to qualified candidates who are not promoted or tenured to make way for an affirmative-action candidate of equal or lesser qualifications;

in effect, nonaffirmative-action candidates must meet a higher standard to gain tenure (Markie 1993). Affirmative action, it may be argued, supports "victims" of past discrimination by discriminating against others. Opponents would contend that reappointment, promotion, and tenure decisions should be based upon merit, not on the basis of a faculty member's race or gender.

Other opponents of affirmative action have contended that it does not benefit women and people of color in the long run. Instead, affirmative action imposes on them a sense of inferiority (Steele 1990) or makes them feel self-hatred and guilt (Rodriguez 1982). Academia values merit above all else, and women and people of color may be perceived as not being qualified to hold faculty positions. Affirmative action, which means to correct past discrimination, may also stigmatize the people it means to benefit*. Banks contended that affirmative action has been linked to a lowering of standards. Women and people of color, no matter how exemplary their training and credentials, "are vulnerable to insinuations that merit was not the main factor in their appointment" (1984, p. 333). He argued that no matter how valuable affirmative action may be, it may be the cause of white hostility and resentment toward people of color and women, thereby resulting in subtle stigmatization.

Faculty members who are not the beneficiaries of affirmative-action programs may believe they are the victims of "reverse discrimination. These faculty members are more likely to challenge affirmative-action plans in court, alleging violations of their civil or constitutional rights. Colleges and universities, especially those not required by a court to implement affirmative-action plans, must balance the need for a diverse faculty with the individual rights of faculty members who are not members of the benefiting groups. This balance involves legal as well as moral and political ramifications.

This report does not dwell on the moral, philosophical, or policy implications of affirmative action. Instead, it focuses on the legal implications. Specifically, affirmative action involves two complex legal questions: To what extent are institutions of higher education legally entitled to use racial

---

*Some may argue that racism and sexism, not affirmative action, stigmatize people of color.

or gender preferences in reappointment, promotion, and tenure decisions; and what are the limits to the use of gender or racial preferences in the reappointment, promotion, and tenure process (Kaplin and Lee 1995)?

The Legal Status of Affirmative Action

The legal status of affirmative action is difficult to gauge today. Congress and a number of state legislatures may make affirmative action illegal in many situations or at least sharply limit its legality in public employment. The Supreme Court justices have been sharply divided and inconsistent in these cases. Furthermore, changes in the composition of the Supreme Court in the nineties are likely to result in different holdings (Kaplin and Lee 1995). Readers should be aware, therefore, that any discussion of the legal principles of affirmative action is subject to become dated as soon as it is written. Nevertheless, affirmative action in certain situations is legal and until (or if) it is made illegal or seriously undermined by the courts or legislatures, an understanding of its principles is important.

In general, the federal government has provided the impetus for affirmative action. Through Title VII and executive orders 11246 and 11375, the federal government has attempted to prohibit discrimination and to eliminate the discriminatory effects of the past. Executive orders 11246 and 11375 have been the major focus of federal affirmative-action initiatives by prohibiting discrimination based upon race, color, religion, gender, and national origin, and requiring federal contractors and subcontractors to develop affirmative-action plans. Institutions also are subject to affirmative-action requirements regarding people with disabilities, disabled veterans, and Vietnam veterans under Section 503 of the Rehabilitation Act and the Vietnam Era Veteran's Readjustment Assistance Act of 1974 (Kaplin and Lee 1995).

Affirmative action was initiated in higher education by the passage of the Equal Employment Opportunity Act of 1972, which imposed specific guidelines for the recruiting and hiring of faculty and staff as a condition for receiving federal financial support (Washington and Harvey 1989). Federal law and initiatives also have provided the impetus for affirmative-action programs in higher education. A recent Supreme Court ruling, however, may endanger a number of federal affirmative-action programs. The Supreme Court recently held in *Adarand Constructors, Inc. vs. Pena* (1995) that governmental affirmative-action programs must be proved to promote "compelling" governmental ends and be "narrowly tailored" to meet those ends* — a very difficult standard. Although this ruling dealt directly with federal contracts programs — and did not deal with affirmative-action plans at colleges and universities — it may affect the requirements of affirmative-action programs imposed on colleges and universities by a number of federal civil-rights laws (see *Chronicle of Higher Education*, June 23, 1995). But affirmative-action initiatives may be in jeopardy at public institutions as well. The Supreme Court refused to grant a University of Maryland appeal of an adverse federal appeals court decision holding that a scholarship for African-Americans violated the 14th Amendment (*Podberesky vs. Kirwan* 1995). These cases, the holding in *Adarand* and its refusal to hear the University of Maryland case, indicate how the current justices on the Supreme Court feel about affirmative action.

Affirmative action is not required unless a court has ordered an institution to eradicate the effects of its own discrimination.

Today, however, affirmative-action programs are legally permitted — sometimes required — to overcome the effects of an institution's own present or past discrimination, and they are less justified when no present or past discrimination is shown (Kaplin and Lee 1995). Affirmative action is not required unless a court has ordered an institution to eradicate the effects of its own discrimination. The issue becomes less clear when institutions voluntarily implement affirmative-action plans to eliminate the effects of societal discrimination or because of an imbalance in the number or percentage of women and people of color in the labor market and in faculty positions.

Affirmative Action and Title VII

Title VII does not require an institution of higher education to give preferential treatment to women or people of color merely because their numbers are low in the faculty ranks. But courts sometimes have required hiring preferences or goals if the reason for the low representation is due to an

---

The court held that all governmental affirmative-action programs will be analyzed using the constitutional standard of "strict scrutiny." In analyzing policy, "strict scrutiny" requires "compelling governmental interests," and the policy must be "narrowly tailored" to meet those interests.

---

institution's own discriminatory practices (Kaplin and Lee 1995). Furthermore, Title VII does not require institutions to point to their own past discriminatory practices to establish voluntary affirmative-action plans for the reappointment, promotion, and tenure of women and people of color. An institution may justify its affirmative-action program on a "manifest imbalance" in the workforce (Clague 1987, p. 250).

Voluntary affirmative-action plans by private colleges and universities are permitted under Title VII. In *Weber vs. Kaiser Aluminum Co.* (1979), the Supreme Court reviewed and upheld a company's plan providing admission to a new skills-training program on the basis of one African-American for every white worker until the proportion of African-Americans in the field reached their proportion in the labor force. A white worker denied admission to the training program claimed that he was the victim of reverse discrimination because he had more seniority than the African-Americans selected. The Supreme Court held that Title VII does not prohibit employers and unions in the *private* sector from *voluntarily* developing affirmative-action plans to end a "*manifest racial imbalance*" in "*traditionally segregated job categories.*"

Kaplin and Lee pointed out several critical factors affecting the outcome in *Weber* (these factors must be satisfied to justify affirmative action in private higher education):

1. There was a "manifest racial imbalance" in the job categories for which the training program had been established;
2. The job category had been traditionally segregated, and rampant discrimination in the past had contributed to the present imbalance;
3. The plan did not "unnecessarily trammel" the interests of white employees (it did not bar white employees from admission to the program); and
4. It was a temporary measure designed to bring African-American representation up to that of the area's workforce (1995, p. 258).

For public institutions, the issue is less clear. They are subject to constitutional restrictions and so are required to overcome the more difficult legal test of "strict scrutiny" in order to establish affirmative-action plans. Nevertheless, public institutions apparently also may be able to establish voluntary affirmative-action plans under Title VII to attract and advance women and people of color in their faculty ranks. In *Johnson vs. Transportation Agency* (1987), the Supreme Court upheld an affirmative-action plan intended to increase the number of women and racial minorities in jobs in which they traditionally were underrepresented. A male employee challenged the promotion of a woman with lesser qualifications. The court applied its reasoning in *Weber* to review the affirmative action in the public sector: There was a "manifest imbalance" in the job category; the plan had not "unnecessarily trammeled" the rights of male employees (they did not have a right to promotion, and they retained their prior employment status); and the plan was temporary (it attained, rather than maintained, a balanced workforce).

Clague indicated that the *Johnson* case settled several issues for employers, including institutions of higher education:

1. Title VII supports voluntary affirmative-action plans at public and private institutions;
2. Preferences may extend to promotion and tenure as well as hiring;
3. The institutions may treat race and gender as "plus" factors in promotion and tenure decisions because there is a "conspicuous imbalance" in this traditionally segregated job category;
4. Exclusive faculty hiring lines for women and people of color likely are unlawful;
5. Quotas, fixed numbers, or fixed percentages probably are unlawful;
6. Affirmative-action plans must be temporary means of combating the effects of discrimination — to attain rather than maintain race and gender balances (1987).

Weber and *Johnson* notwithstanding, the Supreme Court has been sharply divided on the issue of voluntary affirmative-action plans, and colleges and universities should not automatically assume that all of these plans will be upheld in court. Apparently, colleges and universities that can demonstrate a serious underrepresentation of women and people of color in their faculty ranks and that can demonstrate a "manifest imbalance" in the proportion of qualified women and people of color in the labor market and on their faculties may be able to develop affirmative-action plans to remedy this situation (Kaplin and Lee 1995).

The Supreme Court cases upholding such affirmative-action plans, however, have indicated that the proper criterion for proving "manifest imbalance" in professional occupations requiring specific skills is the proportion of qualified candidates in the appropriate labor market. As a result, institutions of higher education may find it very difficult to demonstrate this imbalance because of the small number of people of color who have doctoral degrees and the small number of women who have doctoral degrees in certain fields (Kaplin and Lee 1995).

In *Enright vs. California State University* (1989), an affirmative-action plan calling for gender-conscious hiring was upheld under Title VII. The court determined that the disparity between women who have doctoral degrees in sociology and the proportion of women in the department was a "manifest imbalance," and that the proportion of women in the population (50 percent) and the proportion of women with Ph.D.s in sociology (34 percent) made sociology a "traditionally segregated" field (Kaplin and Lee 1995, p. 270). The court also was persuaded that the plan was a temporary measure, had used goals (not quotas), and that the male who was not hired was not entitled to the position.

In a Title VII case, the faculty member charging reverse discrimination may have to prove that the position is not within a "traditionally segregated job category," and this necessarily involves a historical analysis (Clague 1987, p. 254). People of color are underrepresented at most institutions of higher education (except historically black institutions) and in most fields. Women are underrepresented at many institutions and in many fields. Women and people of color are especially underrepresented in the tenured faculty ranks. Are faculty positions a "traditionally segregated job category"? At many, but certainly not all, institutions, the faculty traditionally have been segregated. Courts have not made it clear whether faculty positions, for affirmative-action purposes, should be subdivided by rank, discipline, or by institutional type (community colleges, state universities, or research institutions, for example) [Clague 1987].

Affirmative-action plans that "unnecessarily trammel" anyone's interests are not likely to be upheld, even if voluntary, temporary, and intended to remedy a "manifest imbalance" in the profession. Although reappointment, promotion, and tenure decisions usually are made on the basis of individual merit and faculty members are not, in theory, competing with each other, situations exist in which a positive decision for one faculty member results in a negative decision for another (for example, where the department is very small or is experiencing budget problems, or in situations in which there is a limit on the percentage of tenured faculty members in a given department). In these situations, institutions must be aware of the potential legal ramifications of their decisions. Since faculty vacancies (or special appointments such as department-chair positions) become available infrequently and on an irregular basis, a decision that the opening should be filled by a woman or person of color may lead to a reverse-discrimination lawsuit by a white male, who effectively may have been "barred" from the position (Kaplin and Lee 1995).

Court-ordered affirmative-action programs are on the most stable legal ground. Such affirmative-action plans have been required of institutions that have been found to have discriminated against women or people of color. For example, in *Palmer vs. District Board of Trustees of St. Petersburg Junior College* (1984), a federal court upheld an affirmative-action plan calling for race-conscious hiring goals because Florida's higher-education system had been found to have discriminated in the past. An African-American male had been selected for a teaching position instead of Palmer, a white male who had been in the position on a temporary basis. Palmer alleged race and age discrimination but did not challenge the affirmative-action plan. Applying the *Weber* test, the court determined that Palmer's interests were not "unnecessarily trammeled" because he was not "reappointed." If, instead, he had been "discharged," the court may have ruled otherwise (Kaplin and Lee 1995, pp. 269-70).

Affirmative action and the Constitution

Constitutional limits on affirmative action stem from the 14th Amendment's Equal Protection Clause and apply to public institutions. Even if federal or state law permits race or gender preferences in faculty employment, the Equal Protection Clause likely would prohibit them unless the public institution is found to have discriminated in the past (Clague 1987; Kaplin and Lee 1995). It is unlikely that the Constitution permits any affirmative-action program that is based on race or gender preferences absent a showing of past or present discrimination.

Although affirmative-action plans may be legally permitted to eliminate the effects of present or past discrimination, the Supreme Court also has implied that some racial preferences may be justified on academic freedom grounds (Clague 1987; Van Alstyne 1993b). In *University of California Regents vs. Bakke* (1978), the Supreme Court invalidated on constitutional grounds the University of California at Davis' affirmative-action program that delegated a certain number of seats in the medical school to students of color. Justice Powell, however, wrote an opinion — in which four other justices agreed — permitting institutions to use race as a positive factor in admission decisions. Powell indicated that the Constitution would permit an institution to strive for a diverse student body. By implication, the Constitution also would permit an affirmative-action plan that increases the diversity of an institution's faculty. Powell stated that the University of California:

> *in arguing that its universities must be accorded the right to select those students who will contribute the most to the robust exchange of ideas ... invokes a countervailing constitutional interest, that of the First Amendment* (p. 313).

Affirmative-action programs giving gender or race preferences in the reappointment, promotion, and tenure of women and people of color probably are constitutionally valid if they are intended to remedy past discrimination. A majority of Supreme Court justices have approved affirmative-action plans intended as remedies for past discrimination in *International Association of Firefighters vs. City of Cleveland* (1986) and *Local 28 of Sheet Metal Workers' International Association vs. EEOC* (1986). *International Association of Firefighters* involved a consent decree calling for race-conscious promotions, and *Sheet Metal Workers* involved access to union membership and its training programs. In *United States vs. Paradise* (1987), the Supreme Court also upheld a court order requiring that 50 percent of promotions to corporal within the Alabama State Troopers be awarded to African-American candidates because they had been systematically excluded over the years, and there had been resistance to court orders (Kaplin and Lee 1995).

Another case illustrating the legal system's approval of racial preferences to remedy past discrimination is *Valentine vs. Smith* (1981). A white female faculty member challenged Arkansas State University's affirmative-action plan after a teaching position she had sought was given to an African-American candidate. She had applied for a position from which she previously had resigned and was the top candidate. But the university, acting on an affirmative-action plan implemented to desegregate the state higher-education system, placed two African-American candidates ahead of her and hired one of them. Valentine sued, alleging that the affirmative-action plan violated the Equal Protection Clause. The court disagreed, holding that racial preferences may be used to remedy the effects of past discrimination.

In upholding the affirmative-action plan the court held that:

1. The affirmative-action plan was designed to attain a balance in the workforce;
2. It lasted only so long as necessary to achieve its goals;
3. Unqualified applicants were not hired; and
4. It did not bar whites from the positions and did not "unnecessarily trammel" their interests (Kaplin and Lee 1995).

Although *Valentine* was a constitutional case, the reasoning by the court paralleled that of the court in *Weber*, a Title VII case. The court in *Valentine* also was persuaded that general societal discrimination led to the underrepresentation in the racial makeup of the faculty (Kaplin and Lee 1995).

In *City of Richmond vs. J.A. Croson* (1989), however, the Supreme Court made it much more difficult for an institution to justify affirmative action under the Equal Protection Clause, and it rejected the argument that general societal discrimination justified explicit race quotas. The court invalidated a program that set aside public construction contracts for minority subcontractors, holding that the Equal Protection Clause of the 14th Amendment required a "strict scrutiny" test for legally justifying race preferences. Under this standard, the program must be shown to serve a "compelling governmental interest" and it must be "narrowly tailored" to meet that interest. This standard of proof is extremely difficult to satisfy, and probably only egregious past discrimination would justify any plan that sets aside a certain number or percentage of positions for women and traditionally underrepresented faculty members. Recently, the Supreme Court made it clear that "strict scrutiny" will apply for governmental affirmative-action programs (see *Adarand Constructors, Inc. vs. Pena* 1995).

Most of the cases previously discussed dealt with hiring, promotions, or advancements. When affirmative-action plans are used in layoffs, the courts have been much less willing to uphold them (Kaplin and Lee 1995) or they will require a demanding standard of justification (Clague 1987). In *Wygant vs. Jackson Board of Education* (1986), the Supreme Court held that an affirmative-action plan containing a retention/layoff provision for public-school teachers of color violated the Equal Protection Clause. The court was concerned that this plan attempted to match the percentage of teachers of color to the percentage of students of color, but it did not invalidate all affirmative-action layoff plans.

Courts no longer will be likely to accept on constitutional grounds a justification based upon general societal discrimination. Title VII affirmative-action cases, therefore, are more likely to succeed in higher education because they permit a showing of "manifest imbalance." And this is more likely to happen at private institutions. Public institutions are subject to constitutional obligations, and plaintiffs likely will frame their arguments in constitutional, not Title VII, terms — making it much more difficult for public institutions to defend their programs.

Nor will courts likely accept affirmative-action plans based upon a need to increase role models for students, especially students of color. This argument was rejected in *Wygant* (Clague 1987). An argument framed in terms of faculty integration (as a result of desegregation), however, has not been explicitly rejected by the Supreme Court. In *Wygant*, the school board attempted to frame its argument in terms of school desegregation rather than employment-discrimination law by characterizing its plan as a "commitment to an effective system of integrated education" (p. 210). This argument could have focused the court on *Brown vs. Board of Education of Topeka* (1954) and other desegregation cases rather than employment-discrimination principles. But the court refused to view this case as a school-desegregation case, leaving open the possibility that such a justification may later validate certain affirmative-action plans. This is unlikely, however, given some of the current justices' suspicion toward (or even opposition to) affirmative-action programs.

To survive the "strict scrutiny" test for race- or gender-conscious policies in reappointment, promotion, and tenure decisions, the Equal Protection Clause would require public institutions to prove past discrimination and that the institution has attempted to remedy the discrimination without race- or gender-conscious policies (Kaplin and Lee 1995). Absent a showing of past discrimination, public institutions are not likely to justify an affirmative-action plan intended to increase the number of underrepresented faculty members.

Title VII, on the other hand, makes it easier for private institutions to justify affirmative-action plans in reappointment, promotion, and tenure policies, especially if they have a history of past discrimination*. The use of quotas, however, probably is unlawful. Although *Weber* permitted the use of quotas by private employers, the Supreme Court in *Johnson* and *Croson* indicated that quotas may be illegal on constitutional and Title VII grounds (Kaplin and Lee 1995). Institutions that use race or gender as a "plus" factor may be able to satisfy the Title VII test more easily. Affirmative-action plans, nevertheless, should be reviewed to ensure that no one's interests are "unnecessarily trammeled" (under Title VII) or that they can survive a "strict scrutiny" test (under the Constitution) [p. 265].

Affirmative action and the faculty contract of employment

Most of this discussion of affirmative action has focused on challenges by faculty members alleging reverse discrimination. Women and people of color may, however, use the language in the contract of employment to require institutions to use race or gender preferences in reappointment, promotion, or tenure decisions. In *Goodman vs. Board of Trustees of Community College District 525* (1981), a court

---

*This would apply to public institutions only if the claims are filed under Title VII — highly unlikely, given recent Supreme Court decisions making it more difficult for public entities to justify affirmative-action initiatives.

held that an employee may prove that the college's affirmative-action program was incorporated in the employment contract, and her failure to receive a promotion was a breach of that contract. Goodman had applied for the position of assistant dean of admissions and records, but instead a younger male was appointed to the position. And in *Sola vs. Lafayette College* (1986), discussed in Section Two, a court held that the college's failure to consider Sola's gender may form the basis for a breach of contract claim.

Institutions should ensure that their institutional documents actually reflect their intentions. In *Scelsa vs. City University of New York* (1992), the university was prevented from relocating its Calendra Italian American Institute and reassigning its director. The director sued under Title VII, claiming that the university's affirmative-action plan, developed two decades earlier, had designated Italian-Americans an underrepresented group among its faculty, and the institution had done little to benefit this group (Kaplin and Lee 1995). The court granted an injunction (a court order preventing the institution from acting as it intended), holding that the university failed to follow its voluntarily adopted affirmative-action plan. Institutions, therefore, should periodically review their policies to ensure that they are protecting (and benefiting) the intended groups.

Southern State University Scenario
Let us return to the Southern State University scenario. Southern State University's affirmative-action program may be legally justified under Title VII and the Equal Protection Clause if the university can show that it indeed is attempting to remedy the effects of its prior discrimination, and that it does not use quotas. In addition, the affirmation plan does not require the promotion or tenure of underrepresented faculty; it merely rewards those schools that promote or tenure those underrepresented faculty members who are qualified. No white male is being replaced or rejected, although departments that have limits on the percentage of tenured faculty members may be subject to discrimination claims if they base their decisions solely upon race.

Title VII also might permit a justification based on the underrepresentation of women and people of color on its faculty if the university can show a "manifest imbalance" in the job market. The proper comparison for determining this imbalance is the percentage of qualified women and people of color in the appropriate job market. This standard might prove extremely difficult for the university since only a small percentage of people of color have the necessary doctorate, and women with Ph.D.s are underrepresented in many fields. But a lawsuit challenging this plan likely would be filed on constitutional grounds, necessitating the application of the "strict scrutiny" test. The Equal Protection Clause probably would not permit an argument based upon a "manifest imbalance." Faculty lines reserved for a woman or person of color may not survive a challenge of reverse discrimination because in effect white males would be barred from qualifying for these positions. Regardless of whether Southern State University's affirmative action is legal, it might be criticized, internally and externally, on moral, philosophical, and political grounds.

The Diversity Dilemma: Balancing Institutional and Individual Rights

Affirmative action in the reappointment, promotion, and tenure process seeks to accomplish three goals: Eliminate the effects of an institution's own present or prior discrimination against women and people of color; remedy societal discrimination and increase the representation of women and people of color in the faculty ranks; and promote racial and gender diversity on college campuses. But as the current debate makes clear, faculty members who do not benefit from affirmative action may believe their individual rights have been violated and that they have been the victims of "reverse discrimination." Institutions of higher education may believe that a balance between the goals of affirmative action and claims of reverse discrimination is impossible to attain, although they should strive to do so.

Courts probably will expect that institutions admit to past discrimination to justify affirmative-action plans. This causes a dilemma for institutions. On the one hand, if institutions confess to past discrimination, they risk litigation from women and people of color for discriminating against them, even if they seek to remedy the situation. If they do not take affirmative action to eliminate the effects of past discrimination, they also may be subject to a lawsuit from women and people of color (see Clague 1987). On the other hand, individuals who are not benefited from their affirmative-action plans also may sue the institutions, claiming reverse discrimination.

Nevertheless, institutions have been able to justify affirmative action if they are attempting to remedy the effects of their own discrimination. In addition, Title VII permits private and public institutions to implement voluntary affirmative-action plans if there is a "manifest imbalance" in the job market; if the plans are only temporary; and if the interests of faculty members not subject to affirmative action are not "trammeled." Public institutions, however, are subject to much stronger standards of justification on constitutional grounds. In today's societal and political climate, the legality of affirmative-action programs are in question, particularly in that these programs were meant to be temporary.

Affirmative action has moral, philosophical, political, financial, and legal implications. We have provided information about the legal implications. This information, however, must be considered tentative since any definitive discussion of the legal implications of affirmative action is impossible. Furthermore, institutions of higher education ultimately must deal with the other implications themselves, taking into account the collective needs and conscience of all of its constituents.

THE LEGAL IMPLICATIONS OF PEER REVIEW

Consider this scenario:

You believe you have been the victim of gender discrimination in your institution's decision not to promote you to full professor. You think that some of the members on the promotion and tenure committee were biased against members of your gender, and you want to know how they voted. You consider filing a claim with the EEOC alleging a Title VII violation. How likely is it that you will obtain the information that you seek?

In 1990, the Supreme Court rejected a claim to an institutional privilege from disclosure of confidential peer-review materials.

In this section, we discuss some of the legal issues associated with peer review, specifically the disclosure of confidential peer-review materials; the liability of administrators and faculty members involved in evaluating candidates for reappointment, promotion, or tenure; and the use of student evaluations and other evaluation tools by peer-review committees.

Colleges and universities rely on the judgments of internal and external peers to assess the quality of a faculty member's scholarship, teaching, and service and to recommend whether reappointment, promotion, or tenure should be granted (Kaplin and Lee 1995). Until recently faculty members usually were not given access to these evaluations, and evaluators were assured of confidentiality. In fact, some evaluators refused to provide candid evaluations unless they were promised confidentiality. During the last 10 years, institutions have been compelled by courts to disclose peer-review materials in the processing of discrimination complaints (Brown and Kurland 1993). Faculty members and administrators involved in the evaluation of unsuccessful candidates for reappointment, promotion, or tenure have been asked to provide depositions, answer interrogatories, or surrender information within their control (Kaplin and Lee 1995).

In 1990, the Supreme Court rejected a claim to an institutional privilege from disclosure of confidential peer-review materials. Prior to 1990, the federal and state courts had been divided regarding this issue. Today, courts generally agree that faculty members charging discrimination can have access to all documentation in their files and perhaps in other faculty members' files as well if the information is relevant to their complaints (Brown and Kurland 1993). The AAUP also has called for disclosure of this material.

In any litigation, each party is allowed to prepare for trial by obtaining information about the other party's case. This information-gathering process is called "discovery." Through discovery, each party can obtain information through depositions, written interrogatories, production of documents, physical or mental examinations, and the like. In a federal discrimination lawsuit, the faculty member alleging discrimination can discover any "nonprivileged" material that is *relevant* to the charges, and this may include peer-review materials. The courts and the Federal Rules of Evidence, which govern discovery in federal litigation, do not favor privileges that keep information confidential. But courts have the authority to recognize privileges on a case-by-case basis (Baglione 1987).

In Title VII cases, the EEOC may be investigating the matter as well. The EEOC's discovery rights are broader than those of individual faculty members. This is because Congress wanted the EEOC to have extensive access to evidence to eradicate employment discrimination (Barrow 1990). Courts also have construed the relevancy requirement very broadly in EEOC investigations, thereby allowing access to a great deal of peer-review materials which might provide evidence of discrimination (Baglione 1987). If an institution refuses to disclose the peer-review materials, the EEOC has the authority to issue a subpoena and to sue the institution in federal court to enforce the subpoena (Barrow 1990).

Arguments For and Against Disclosure of Peer-Review Materials

Faculty members challenging a negative employment decision and the EEOC investigating charges of discrimination must rely on access to confidential peer-review materials, prompting institutions to argue that this information must be privileged against disclosure to ensure the integrity of the peer-review system (Baglione 1987). Institutions often claim that maintaining the confidentiality of peer-review evaluations is essential because the promotion and tenure process needs candid evaluations from reviewers, and this can only be accomplished when evaluators are assured of confidentiality.

In addition to maintaining the integrity of the peer-review system, institutions have requested a qualified privilege to keep peer-review materials confidential on the grounds that liberal discovery rules allow faculty members or the EEOC to demand production of too many documents relating to reappointment, promotion, or tenure evaluations, and this production will have disruptive and burdensome effects on institutions (Baglione 1987). Furthermore, when a faculty member seeks access to the personnel files of other faculty members for comparison, the disclosure may cause "bad blood" in the department, embarrassment to others, and damage the reputations of faculty members not involved in the lawsuit (see *Chronicle of Higher Education*, Feb. 3, 1995).

Colleges and universities also have claimed a privilege protecting the confidentiality of peer-review materials on constitutional grounds. Institutions have argued that the peer-review system serves important academic freedom interests. The Supreme Court recognized the First Amendment right of institutional academic freedom in *Sweezy vs. New Hampshire* (1957) and *Keyishian vs. Board of Regents* (1967). Academic freedom includes the right of colleges and universities to decide, on academic grounds, who may teach. The process of deciding who may teach necessarily requires the reappointment, promotion, or tenure process, and to maintain the integrity of this process, confidentiality is needed to ensure that evaluators are candid (Olswang and Lee 1992; *School Law Reporter*, December 1994). Confidential peer review, therefore, serves important academic freedom interests.

There also are arguments in favor of disclosing peer-review materials. Faculty members who believe they have been discriminated against are able to determine whether they have a legal claim if they have access to this information. Also, evaluators should be held accountable to the institution and to the faculty members involved by disclosing their evaluations (see Coates 1995). Faculty members also should have the same rights as many employees in nonacademic public organizations, who have the right in a number of states to inspect their personnel records (see Olswang and Lee 1992). Furthermore, disclosing this information to the faculty member on request actually may avoid potential lawsuits, since the faculty member may find that the reasons for the negative decision are valid. Finally, disclosure of this information forces evaluators to be honest and forthright (Coates 1995), and encourages them to base their decisions upon specific examples to avoid the possibility of being charged with discrimination.

Some scholars also have questioned the need for an academic freedom privilege (see DeLano 1987). These scholars have contended that the academic freedom to decide who may teach means only that institutions may determine who may teach *on academic grounds*. A decision based upon discrimination or one that censors free speech is not entitled to constitutional protection, and the only way to determine whether the institution's decision is based upon academic grounds is to examine the materials used to make the decisions. A privilege keeping peer-review materials confidential may give colleges and universities more than the freedom to decide who may teach; it also gives them the freedom to base their decisions upon any grounds, including discrimination or political or religious affiliation and other illegal grounds.

Despite the arguments in favor of protecting peer-review materials from being disclosed to faculty members challenging negative reappointment, promotion, or tenure decisions, the current judicial trend allows faculty members access to this information, especially in employment-discrimination litigation.

Peer Review and the Courts — A Short History

In 1990, the Supreme Court decided that at least as far the EEOC was concerned institutions of higher education could not claim a privilege of confidentiality in discrimination cases. In *University of Pennsylvania vs. E.E.O.C.* (1990), the Supreme Court upheld the EEOC's subpoena of various peer-review materials. Prior to this case, courts were divided on the issue of whether academic institutions enjoyed a privilege protecting confidential peer evaluations from disclosure. The Supreme Court made it clear that such a privilege could not be available to frustrate the EEOC's obligation to eradicate discrimination in faculty employment. Today, courts seem fairly consistent in giving access to peer-review materials in cases alleging discrimination (Hendrickson 1991).

Before the *University of Pennsylvania* case, federal courts dealt with requests for disclosure of peer-review materials by faculty members or the EEOC in three ways: They granted a qualified privilege protecting such materials; they balanced the academic freedom and educational-excellence interests against the need to fairly investigate charges of discrimination; or they rejected any institutional argument in favor of disclosure. Following is a summary of some of the major cases dealing with this issue.

The first major case dealing with the disclosure of peer-review materials was *In Re Dinnan* (1981), which rejected such a privilege. In this case, James Dinnan, a member of the College of Education's Promotion Review Committee at the University of Georgia, refused to answer questions regarding how he voted on a promotion application. Dinnan appealed his conviction, claiming an academic freedom privilege*. The Court of Appeals for the Fifth Circuit held that no such privilege existed, stating that academic freedom, though important, cannot cause other interests (eradicating employment discrimination or freedom of speech, for example) to be frustrated.

In *Gray vs. Board of Higher Education, City of New York* (1982), the Court of Appeals for the Second Circuit held that the decision of whether to disclose confidential peer-review materials requires a balancing of competing interests. An African-American instructor at LaGuardia Community College's business division denied promotion to assistant professor on several occasions asked the court to compel two members of the personnel committee (one of whom was the chair of his department) to disclose how they voted in his case (the faculty members claimed an academic freedom privilege). Concerned that Gray would not be able to prove intentional discrimination without knowing how these faculty members voted, the court adopted the AAUP's solution of a balancing test, taking into consideration factors including whether the candidate received a meaningful statement of reasons from the peer-review committee and was afforded proper intramural grievance procedures. The court believed this solution struck an appropriate balance between academic freedom and an individual's right to fair

---

*His contempt conviction included a $100 fine for each day he refused to disclose his vote. After 30 days, if he remained defiant of the order to disclose his vote, he would receive a 90-day jail sentence.

consideration on the other. In this case, the court tipped the balance toward discovery.

Although the court in *Gray* held in favor of disclosure, it indicated that if the institution provided an unsuccessful tenure candidate with a meaningful statement of reasons, that factor would weigh heavily in balancing whether to protect the committee members' votes and other peer-review materials from disclosure. In *E.E.O.C. vs. University of Notre Dame Du Lac* (1983), the Court of Appeals for the Seventh Circuit took a stronger stance in protecting peer-review material from disclosure by holding that colleges and universities had a qualified privilege against disclosure of peer-review materials. The EEOC had attempted to obtain peer-review materials in a race-discrimination claim. The court stressed the importance of confidentiality in the peer-review process and held that before producing the files to the EEOC, the university should be permitted to redact all identifying information, and the release of further information must be based on a finding of "compelling need."

The Court of Appeals for the Third Circuit, however, rejected the qualified-privilege argument and the balancing test. In *E.E.O.C. vs. Franklin and Marshall College* (1985), the EEOC sought enforcement of a subpoena for a number of documents in a national-origin discrimination claim, including tenure-recommendation forms prepared by faculty members; annual evaluations; letters of reference; evaluations of the faculty member's publications by outside experts; and all notes, letters, memoranda, and materials considered during the tenure decision. The court, acknowledging the potential burden on the peer-review process, held in favor of the EEOC, noting that since Congress did not exempt academic institutions from Title VII's prohibition against discrimination, they were subject to EEOC investigations.

Courts appeared to move away from granting a qualified privilege against disclosure of peer-review materials. In *Jackson vs. Harvard University* (1986)*, the court held the faculty member was not entitled to discover the identities of evaluators without showing a "particularized need" sufficient to overcome the university's qualified academic freedom

---

*This case finally was decided in 1990 and was discussed in Section Four.

privilege, nor was she entitled to discover information regarding the selection of students and nonfaculty employees or the tenure decisions of faculty members at other schools in the university. The court held, however, that she was entitled to additional information not found in the affirmative-action reports, the information regarding tenure candidates for the past 10 years, including the tenure files of men granted tenure during that period (with the names redacted), and the records of complaints by business-school faculty members.

The *Jackson* court acknowledged the existence of the qualified privilege, but such a privilege was rejected by a New Jersey Court in *Dixon vs. Rutgers* (1987). Dixon, an African-American female assistant professor in the College of Arts and Sciences, was denied tenure because of what she claimed was gender discrimination. Dixon requested information contained in her promotion and tenure file. The court held that academic freedom privilege did not protect the confidentiality of material contained in promotion packets of faculty members of the state university in the face of a gender-discrimination challenge. In *Orbovich vs. Macalester College* (1988), a court ordered the disclosure of the comparative evidence (the personnel files of other faculty members) because that evidence is relevant in a case alleging gender discrimination and rejected the college's argument that the production of this material was too burdensome, holding that the college must prove that the burden was "unreasonable." Nevertheless, the court recognized the confidential nature of the personnel files and issued a protective order that barred further disclosure without court approval.

As these cases indicate, the federal courts were not in agreement regarding the disclosure of peer-review materials. Some scholars argued that the lack of harmony among the courts created problems for academic decisionmakers who lacked the security of assured confidentiality before making candid appraisals (see Partain 1987). This lack of agreement and the ensuing confusion for the institutions, faculty members alleging discrimination, and the EEOC led the Supreme Court to accept the appeal of *University of Pennsylvania*, which had been ordered by the lower federal courts to turn over peer-review materials to the EEOC in a complaint alleging gender and national-origin discrimination.

University of Pennsylvania vs. E.E.O.C. (1990)

In *University of Pennsylvania*, the university asked the Supreme Court to hold that academic institutions had a qualified privilege against disclosure of confidential peer-review materials. Although the privilege was specifically requested in Title VII cases, it probably also would apply to other situations in which faculty members were denied reappointment, promotion, or tenure, including violations of academic freedom, breach of contract, and other such litigation (see Rabban 1993).

In 1985, the University of Pennsylvania denied tenure to Rosalie Tung, an associate professor in the Wharton School of Business. Tung filed a Title VII discrimination claim with the EEOC, alleging gender and national-origin discrimination. She stated in her charge that she had been sexually harassed by her department chairman and that after she insisted their relationship remain professional, he submitted a negative letter to the university's personnel committee. She also claimed that her qualifications were "equal to or better than" those of five named male faculty members who had received more favorable treatment. Tung noted that faculty members in her department had recommended her for tenure; that she had been given no reason for the decision against her; and that she had discovered that the personnel committee attempted to justify its decision "on the ground that the Wharton School is not interested in China-related research," which she claimed meant that the school did not want a "Chinese-American, Oriental woman in their school" (p. 184).

The EEOC undertook an investigation into the charge and requested a variety of information from the university. When the university refused to provide some of the information, the EEOC issued a subpoena seeking, among other elements, Tung's tenure-review file and the tenure files of the five male faculty members identified in the charge. The university contended that certain items in the subpoena were "confidential peer-review information," specifically, confidential letters written by Tung's evaluators; the chairperson's letter of evaluation; documents reflecting the internal deliberations of the tenure committees; and comparable portions of the tenure-review files of the five males. When the university refused to comply with the subpoena, the EEOC sued to enforce its subpoena. The lower federal courts ordered the university to comply with the subpoena, and the Supreme Court accepted the university's appeal.

The university contended that the EEOC should be required to seek a judicial finding of "particularized necessity," beyond a showing of mere relevance, before the peer-review materials are disclosed (essentially what the court in *University of Notre Dame Du Lac* [1983] had decided). To support this request, the university raised essentially two claims. First, it urged the court to recognize a qualified common-law privilege against disclosure of confidential peer-review materials. This assertion was grounded in the Federal Rules of Evidence permitting courts to recognize privileges on a case-by-case basis. The university claimed that this privilege was necessary to protect the integrity of the peer-review process, which in turn is central to the proper functioning of colleges and universities. The Supreme Court refused to recognize such a privilege because Congress had considered these concerns but did not provide the privilege. By extending Title VII to institutions of higher education and providing broad EEOC subpoena powers, the court reasoned, Congress did not see fit to create a privilege for peer-review materials. Furthermore, to enable the EEOC to make informed decisions at each stage of the enforcement process, Title VII confers a broad right of access to relevant peer-review materials. At the same time, Title VII had provisions preventing the EEOC from making confidential materials public. The Supreme Court noted that:

> *disclosure of peer-review materials will be necessary in order for the [EEOC] to determine whether illegal discrimination has taken place. Indeed, if there is a "smoking gun" to be found that demonstrates discrimination in tenure decisions, it is likely to be tucked away in peer-review files* (p. 584).

Imposing a requirement on the EEOC that it demonstrate a specific reason for disclosure beyond a showing of mere relevance, the court reasoned, would place a substantial litigation-producing obstacle in the way of the EEOC's efforts to investigate and remedy alleged discrimination; a university faced with disclosure might use the privilege to frustrate the EEOC's mission. The Supreme Court was reluctant to place a potent weapon in the hands of employers who have no interest in complying voluntarily with the act and who wish instead to delay investigations by the EEOC.

The Supreme Court also rejected the University of Pennsylvania's second claim: that it had a First Amendment right of academic freedom against wholesale disclosure of the contested documents. The university contended that it exercises the right of determining, on academic grounds, who may teach through the process of awarding tenure. The peer-review process is the most important element of the tenure system, and it requires candid and detailed evaluations from internal and external reviewers. Because evaluators traditionally have been provided with assurances of confidentiality to ensure candor, requiring disclosure of peer-review evaluations without compelling reasons would undermine the tenure process, thereby infringing on academic freedom. Furthermore, the university claimed that disclosure of this information would result in a "chilling effect" on candid evaluations and, as a result, the quality of the evaluations would decline and tenure committees no longer would be able to rely on them. Disclosure of peer-review materials also will lead to divisiveness and tension among the faculty, placing a strain on faculty relations and impairing the "free exchange of ideas" that is the "hallmark of academic freedom" (pp. 585-6).

The Supreme Court disagreed. First, it believed that the university's argument was misplaced. The cases ensuring a First Amendment right to academic freedom involved governmental attempts to control or direct the content of the speech engaged in by the university or those affiliated with it. The EEOC was not attempting to regulate the content of the university's speech; it was not providing criteria the university must use in selecting faculty members, nor was it preventing the university from using any criteria it wished, except those prohibited by Title VII. The court determined that the university's claim "did not fit neatly within any right of academic freedom," and what the university sought was an expanded right of academic freedom.

The court also rejected the university's contentions regarding the impact of disclosure on the peer-review process, referring to these arguments as "extremely attenuated," "remote," and "speculative." The court, in other words, was not convinced that disclosure would undermine academic freedom or the peer-review process, noting that confidentiality is not the norm in all peer-review systems, and that some disclosure also would take place if the university's request was adopted. Furthermore, the court was not convinced that academicians would be less candid or honest in evaluating candidates for reappointment, promotion, or tenure:

> *Finally, we are not so ready as [the university] seems to be to assume the worst about those in the academic community. Although it is possible that some evaluators may become less candid as the possibility of disclosure increases, others may simply ground their evaluations in specific examples and illustrations in order to deflect potential claims of bias or unfairness. Not all academics will hesitate to stand up and be counted when they evaluate their peers* (p. 588).

It can be argued that this ruling is limited to the specific issue before the court: whether the EEOC in a Title VII investigation was required to show a "particularized necessity" to have access to tenure-review files rather than merely demonstrating that the information was "relevant" to its investigation (Olswang and Lee 1992; *School Law Reporter*, December 1994, p. 2). Furthermore, few faculty members actually will find in these materials the type of information they need to conclusively prove discrimination, and courts are highly deferential to academic decisions anyway, especially if the peer-review committees voted against reappointment, promotion, or tenure (Olswang and Lee 1992).

Nevertheless, the *University of Pennsylvania* case is important because it appears to permit access to confidential peer-review materials upon the filing of an EEOC complaint, and it gives the EEOC the right to discover confidential information contained in other faculty members' files. Clearly, colleges and universities no longer can assure peer evaluators total confidentiality, and they should guarantee that these evaluations are well documented and supported by ample evidence (Olswang and Lee 1992). Furthermore, even though this case involved an EEOC subpoena, faculty plaintiffs also are likely to be entitled to peer-review information, including letters from outside evaluators, written recommendations of departmental or other committees, and other relevant information (Kaplin and Lee 1995).

....colleges and universities no longer can assure peer evaluators total confidentiality, and they should guarantee that these evaluations are well documented and supported by ample evidence.

This case also is indicative of the courts' belief that the interest in preventing discrimination outweighs the institutions' interests in keeping peer-review information confidential. Many scholars still believe that disclosure of confidential peer-review materials will prevent candid evaluations of candidates, an argument the Supreme Court rejected by indicating that potential disclosure will only force evaluators to provide specific examples in support of their recommendations. Regardless, courts are reluctant to privilege this information in discrimination cases, believing that if any evidence of discrimination exists, it is likely to be found in peer-review materials. Research indicates, however, that in the few cases in which faculty members prevailed in discrimination cases, the information contained in peer-review files was not vital to the resolution of the cases (Olswang and Lee 1992). Furthermore, the research does not support the perception that granting greater access to peer-review materials will significantly increase the tenure rates at many colleges and universities (Bednash 1991).

Some scholars believe the University of Pennsylvania's academic freedom claim, if accepted, would have actually hindered academic freedom. Frost contended that the university's insistence on a confidential peer-review process actually works against academic freedom (1991). Academic freedom, Frost argued, was developed within the context of individual rights and stressed the importance of open and free inquiry, and it was:

> *convoluted to structure the tenure process so as to restrict open debate and inquiry on the assumption that an open process might reduce candor, and then use academic freedom doctrine to support that logic. A confidential peer-review process makes open debate impossible because it restricts relevant information, and thus free exchange, to a limited group of scholars. A more open procedure, with participants expressing and supporting responsible opinions, would seem to be more in harmony with the scholarly mission of the university* (p. 349).

Access to committee deliberations and actual votes
Faculty members have been given access to promotion and tenure committee deliberations and the actual votes of

reviewers. *In Re Dinnan* (1981) dealt with this very issue, and the court indicated very little patience for an argument claiming that disclosure of a promotion and tenure vote would undermine the peer-review process, and for those who claim such a privilege:

> *No one compelled Professor Dinnan to take part in the tenure decision process. Persons occupying positions of responsibility, like Dinnan, often must make difficult decisions. The consequence of such responsibility is that occasionally the decisionmaker will be called upon to explain his actions. In such a case, he must have the courage to stand up and publicly account for his decision. If that means that a few weak-willed individuals will be deterred from serving in positions of public trust, so be it; society is better off without their services. If the decision-maker has acted for legitimate reasons, he has nothing to fear. We find nothing heroic or noble about [Dinnan's] position; we see only an attempt to avoid responsibility for his actions. If [Dinnan] was unwilling to accept responsibility for his actions, he should never have taken part in the tenure decision-making process. However, once he accepted such a role of public trust, he subjected himself to explaining to the public and any affected individual his decisions and the reasons behind them* (p. 432).

Some courts have denied access to committee deliberations or the actual votes of committee members. For example, in *Desimone vs. Skidmore College* (1987), the court refused to grant the faculty member access to committee deliberations because the committee twice had ruled in the faculty member's favor, and it was the dean who denied the faculty member tenure. Despite *Desimone*, courts have been willing to grant access to these materials because they are considered necessary to sustain charges of discrimination. In *Gray* (1982), discussed previously, the court determined that disclosure of committee members' votes was necessary in light of the institution's refusal to provide meaningful reasons for a negative promotion decision. In the *Franklin and Marshall College* (1985) case, the court granted access to this material citing *In Re Dinnan* as persuasive. In *Jackson* (1986), the court granted access to the deliberations of the tenure committee. And in *University of Pennsylvania* (1990), the Supreme Court indicated that such information should be available to the EEOC if it determines it to be relevant.

Committee members who refuse to disclose their votes when ordered by a court face the same consequences that Dinnan faced: a contempt citation, fines, and jail time. In an interesting note, despite the ruling in the case Dinnan still refused to disclose how he voted, and the court ordered him jailed; he arrived at the jail dressed in full academic regalia (Kaplin and Lee 1995).

Alternatives to full disclosure

The Federal Rules of Evidence also permit courts to issue protective orders that protect a party from annoyance, embarrassment, oppression, or undue burden or expense (Barrow 1990). Even if the institution must disclose peer-review information, it may seek a court order allowing limited disclosure. A protective order, for example, may allow the institution to redact the files or to limit access to those individuals directly involved in the litigation (Barrow 1990; DeLano 1987; Partain 1987; Weeks 1990). A protective order allows faculty members a fair opportunity to prove their charges but not be too broad.

The *University of Pennsylvania* case did not address the issue of whether identifying information can be redacted. Colleges and universities may be able to redact the names and any identifying information of peer reviewers before permitting the EEOC access to the files. Therefore, a de facto qualified privilege still may exist (Frost 1991). Although, as Kaplin and Lee pointed out, the court's language upholding the EEOC's need for "relevant" information suggests that if the EEOC asserts that the identifying information is relevant, access would have to be provided (1995).

Redaction might serve the purposes of all parties in a discrimination litigation (Barrow 1990): The faculty member and the EEOC would have access to the evaluations, and the institution still would protect the identities of the reviewers, maintaining some level of confidentiality. Furthermore, one can argue that the identities of reviewers are irrelevant in a discrimination lawsuit. The identities of external reviewers may be particularly irrelevant because even if there is proof of discrimination in these evaluations, it is the institution, not the reviewers, who actually make the decision (see Baglione 1987).

Redaction, though arguably preferable to full disclosure, does not solve all the problems. As Barrow indicated, faculty members in small departments probably would identify the evaluator by the writing style, handwriting, or print type of a document (1990). Redaction, therefore, may not protect the identity of reviewers in all cases. Furthermore, colleges and universities may redact more than the identities of reviewers, making discrimination more difficult to prove. On occasion the EEOC may be able to argue that redaction is useless; this is particularly true if the faculty member believes that specific people intentionally discriminated against him or her, and the faculty member's attorney wishes to interrogate them.

Courts are reluctant to allow institutions to protect peer-review information when allegations of discrimination are made. Since the Supreme Court has made it clear that no common-law or academic freedom privilege exists, an institution's only recourse may be a state law protecting the disclosure of this kind of information. As we will discuss in the next section, some states provide some protection, but many states do not. Institutions wishing to avoid disclosure of confidential peer-review materials may have to lobby their state legislators for statutory protection (Barrow 1990).

State Law and the Peer-Review System

For many public institutions (and some private ones as well), *University of Pennsylvania* has little significance since their states' laws have been interpreted to permit access to personnel files. Administrators and faculty members involved in the reappointment, promotion, and tenure process should understand the extent to which their states protect confidential peer-review materials. Many states have employee "right-to-know" laws which grant employees the right to inspect their personnel files. These laws, however, usually exempt "reference letters." Many states also have open records laws (often referred to as "sunshine laws") which permit access to public documents unless the documents are exempted from disclosure. One exemption might be personal information which, if disclosed, would violate an employee's right to privacy (see Olswang and Lee 1992).

Employee right-to-know laws

Employee right-to-know laws have been used successfully to gain access to a faculty member's personnel file. For example, the state of Pennsylvania's law guaranteeing faculty members the right to inspect their personnel files was used successfully in two 1988 cases to gain access to peer-review materials. In *Pennsylvania State University vs. Commonwealth of Pennsylvania, Department of Labor and Industry, Bureau of Labor Standards* (1988), the court held that the Pennsylvania Personnel Files Act requiring the disclosure of "performance evaluations" includes tenure reports. Although the law exempted "letters of reference," the court determined that tenure reviews are performance evaluations. Also in *Lafayette College vs. Commonwealth of Pennsylvania, Department of Labor and Industry, Bureau of Labor Standards* (1988), the court determined that a faculty member denied tenure was entitled not only to his tenure file but also to the letters by external scholars evaluating a manuscript authored by the faculty member. The bureau determined that these materials were performance evaluations. The court upheld that bureau's determination and rejected the college's arguments that the tenure reports and the letters of evaluation were "letters of reference" and thus exempted from the Personnel Files Act.

In other states, these cases may be decided differently. For example, in *Muskovitz vs. Lubbers* (1990), a Michigan court exempted some peer evaluations from disclosure, ruling that a letter from a dean to the provost regarding a faculty member's performance was exempt from the state's right-to-know act (Kaplin and Lee 1995). The court characterized the letter as a "staff planning document," one of the exemptions to the law. It also ruled that the names of people who prepared the evaluations, and other identifying information, were exempt from the law as "employee references supplied to the employer" and could be redacted from the documents submitted to the faculty member (Kaplin and Lee, p. 336).

In California, faculty members would have a more difficult time gaining access to their personnel files. In *Scharf vs. Regents of the University of California* (1991), six faculty members denied tenure and promotion and the American Federation of Teachers sued the University of California claiming that the state's Education Code gave faculty members complete access to their personnel files. The court held that given the University of California's constitutional autonomy, the state's right-to-know law was inapplicable. The court also held that faculty members involved in the peer-review process had a state constitutional right to privacy — in effect, the right to privacy protected peer-review materials from disclosure. Furthermore, the court was persuaded that the faculty members were provided with a comprehensive summary of the peer-review material.

As indicated in *Scharf,* a state's right-to-privacy laws may protect peer-review materials from disclosure, but this right is not absolute. In *Board of Trustees vs. Superior Court* (1981), the court denied a former Stanford professor's request to inspect the personnel records of certain faculty members on the ground that the professor had not demonstrated sufficient relevance or necessity outweighing the faculty members' constitutional guarantee of privacy. The court indicated, however, that legitimate claims of discrimination or violations of free speech may provide the "necessity" outweighing other faculty members' right to privacy.

Allegations of defamation or other torts do not outweigh the right to privacy. In *Kahn vs. Superior Court of the County of Santa Clara* (1987), Ivor Davies was denied the McDonnell Chair of East European History by the history department at Stanford University, even though a search committee had recommended him for the position. The provost agreed to provide Davies with a written summary of the grounds for the decision, but Davies filed a defamation lawsuit against Kahn (who was a department faculty member), other faculty members of the history department, and unnamed people who submitted references to the committee. Davies sought to have Kahn and others disclose how they voted, the motives for the votes, and the contents of comments made during a faculty meeting (during which Davies claimed he was defamed). The court found that California's right to privacy protected Kahn and the peer-review files from discovery. California's right to privacy, the court held, protects against both public and private invasions of privacy, but it is qualified — courts will not enforce the right against compelling state interests that outweigh the right to privacy (torts such as defamation are not compelling enough, but violations of constitutional or civil rights might be). The court also was convinced that Davies was sufficiently provided with a comprehensive summary of the reasons for the denial.

Employee right-to-know laws, therefore, guarantee faculty members in some states access to their personnel records, which may contain confidential peer-review materials. In some states, however, the right to privacy (of peer reviewers) may prevent faculty members challenging a negative reappointment, promotion, or tenure decision from having access to confidential peer-review materials. But even in these states, the right to privacy may be outweighed by legitimate claims of constitutional or civil rights. In all cases, institutions should provide faculty members with a comprehensive summary of the reasons for the decision.

State sunshine laws

Faculty members also have used state open-records laws to gain access not only to their files but to the files of other faculty members to determine whether they were treated fairly in an employment decision. Some state courts have interpreted these statutes as permitting access to the substance of the peer-review decision, although the names and other identifying information of the reviewers may be protected from disclosure in some states (Olswang and Lee 1992).

In *State Ex Rel. James vs. Ohio State University* (1994), the Supreme Court of Ohio held that materials contained in promotion and tenure files maintained by the university are public records subject to disclosure under the Ohio Public Records Act. William Calvin James, an assistant professor in the department of geological sciences, sought access to and copies of records contained in promotion and tenure files maintained by the university. The dean of the college of math and physical sciences offered James access to a redacted version of James' own promotion and tenure file but refused him access to any other faculty member's file. The dean also refused to provide James with access to the chairperson's evaluation letter and any information that might reveal the identity of persons evaluating James' work. James sued to compel disclosure of the disputed information.

The university claimed that the records should be redacted to protect the evaluators' names, and that disclosure would substantially infringe on the university's constitutionally protected right to academic freedom. The court rejected the university's academic freedom argument essentially for the same reasons that the U.S. Supreme Court did in *University of Pennsylvania*; specifically, the court determined that the issue was not whether the university is permitted to decide on academic grounds who receives promotion and tenure but whether the *records* of those decisions are public. The court rejected the argument that the integrity of the peer-review system would be undermined by a faculty member's access to personnel files. The court noted that scholars routinely evaluate each other's work in such public forums as conferences and journals, but even if the system is undermined by disclosure of peer-review materials, this was a matter for the legislature to correct, not the courts. The court also noted:

> *In addition, it is ironic that the university here argues that academic freedom is challenged by the disclosure of the documents. It seems the antithesis of academic freedom to maintain secret files upon which promotion and tenure decisions are made, unavailable even to the person who is the subject of the evaluation.*

The *James* decision is important. The court was strongly in favor of disclosure of promotion and tenure files, and this has been the trend in recent years. This case also may have granted more rights to faculty members in Ohio than those required by the *University of Pennsylvania* case. Actually, this case is striking because it allows public access to public university files (anyone can review these files because they are available under the state's sunshine act). Furthermore, not only does this case hold that faculty members are entitled to see unredacted versions of their own promotion and tenure files (an issue the Supreme Court did not address), but it also suggests that they may be entitled to see the files of their colleagues as well (*School Law Reporter*, December 1994). *James* also highlights the "delicate balancing that must be kept between the interests of individual professors and the general public in disclosure of public documents and the interests of universities in ensuring the integrity of their promotion and tenure processes" (p. 3). Whether other states follow the reasoning of the Ohio Supreme Court, of course, remains to be seen.

A college or university facing either a request for disclosure of peer-review materials or a request to keep those documents confidential should review certain internal documents prior to acting on the request. For example, many faculty collective-bargaining agreements may contain provisions relating to personnel records and evaluations. In addition, the internal policies, rules, and regulations of the institution may set forth obligations with regard to the retention and disclosure of personnel records.

The current trend in courts is toward disclosure. Even the AAUP, which previously had contended that a qualified privilege can be invoked on a balancing of factors, including access to a statement of meaningful reasons and review procedures, issued a report calling for broad disclosure in litigation as well as internal reviews. The 1992 report, "Access to Faculty Personnel Files," reaches the following conclusions:

1. Faculty members should have access to their own files, including unredacted letters, at all times;
2. Faculty members should be afforded access upon request to general information about other faculty members such as is normally contained in a curriculum vitae;
3. Files of a faculty complainant and of other faculty members, for purposes of comparison, should be available in unredacted form to faculty appeals committees to the extent such committees deem the information relevant and necessary to the fair disposition of the case before them; and
4. A faculty appeals committee should make available to the aggrieved faculty member, in unredacted form and without prejudging the merits of the case, all materials it deems relevant to the complaint, including personnel files of other faculty members, having due regard for the privacy of those who are not parties to the complaint (*Academe*, July/August 1992).

Student Evaluations and Other Evaluation Tools Used by Peer-Review Committees

Reappointment, promotion, and tenure decisions usually are based upon the quality of a candidate's scholarship, service, and teaching, which is determined largely through judgments of many people. Many negative tenure decisions are based on deficient scholarship, which often is measured in terms of the number and quality of publications. Some negative decisions are based upon inadequate service commitments. Although some aspect of the service criteria (the number of commitments, for example) can be quantified, this also can be subjective (whether service on an institutionwide committee is more important than on a department committee, for example).

Poor teaching also is a common basis for a negative decision — probably more so in recent years. But what constitutes effective or ineffective teaching is highly subjective as well. Institutions, however, often attempt to measure teaching through observations, portfolios, or student evaluations (see Centra 1993 for a discussion of the research on the validity, reliability, and utility of these measures). Student evaluations, in particular, increasingly are being used in tenure and promotion. The ease of obtaining these data and the extensive research supporting their use have, no doubt, contributed to their acceptance.

Student evaluations, in particular, increasingly are being used in tenure and promotion.

Despite the subjectivity of measuring the quality of a faculty member's scholarship, service, and teaching accomplishments, courts will rarely, if ever, question the appropriateness of an institution's criteria (or how they measure them) for granting reappointment, promotion, or tenure. Peer-review committees have great discretion in how they measure these criteria and what weight they give to each criterion. Courts hold that faculty members and administrators involved in the peer-review process are experts, and they will rarely substitute their judgments for those of peer-review committees*. Peer-review committees, therefore, may evaluate faculty candidates using student evaluations, observations, portfolios, citation counts, external evaluators, and other information. Although these evaluation tools all have strengths and weaknesses (see Centra 1993), peer-review committees may use them as they see fit — so long as they do not violate the candidates' civil, constitutional, or contractual rights.

Faculty members who challenge an institution's reliance on a particular evaluation tool rarely succeed. Course content, teaching methods, grading, and classroom behavior all involve issues of academic freedom (see Section Three), and courts often determine that they are not qualified to make a better judgment than peer-review committees even if these

---

*Although juries may have less deference (Lee 1995).

matters were not protected by academic freedom (see Kaplin and Lee 1995). In *Wirsing vs. Board of Regents of the University of Colorado* (1990), a tenured professor of education refused to administer the university's standardized course-evaluation forms for her classes, and the dean of the department denied her a pay increase because of her refusal. The professor sued to have the university grant her the pay increase and to prevent it from requiring her to use the form, alleging that the university was violating her academic freedom. The court rejected her argument, holding that although the professor had a right to disagree with the university about the use of standardized evaluation forms, she had no right to fail to perform a duty imposed upon her as a condition of employment. Because she had a right to openly criticize the use of such forms and the university's requirement was unrelated to course content, the court found that the institution did not violate her academic freedom (Kaplin and Lee 1995).

There have been studies indicating that women and people of color may be evaluated lower than white males (in student evaluations, for example), thus creating the possibility of a disparate-impact claim. The research in this area, however, has been inconsistent (Centra 1993). Although this area of study deserves more attention, there are no legal obstacles to the use of any evaluation tool. And the inconsistency of the research will make it unlikely that a court will sustain such a claim of disparate impact.

So long as peer-review committees do not act arbitrarily and use the evaluation tools consistently and fairly, courts are unlikely to interfere. Institutions, however, should use multiple methods for evaluation (see Gillmore 1983). And evaluators should be trained to judge effectively and to use specific and detailed examples for their decisions.

Defamation Liability and Other Claims
Against Peer-Review Evaluators

Administrators and faculty members involved in the peer-review process may be sued for defamation for comments made during an evaluation, and some administrators may be held personally liable for the violation of a faculty member's contractual, civil, or constitutional rights. Probably, the most common tort claim against peer reviewers is defamation. A defamation is an intentionally or recklessly false published or spoken communication that injures another person's reputation or good name (*Black's Law Dictionary* 1991). There are two types of defamation claims: slander (the communication is spoken) and libel (the communication is published in writing or broadcast in some manner through the electronic media). Since the statement in a defamation must be false, the faculty member bringing the lawsuit must prove falsity. Truth is a defense for those accused of defamation.

The communication must be serious enough that it would injure the faculty member's reputation, and it must be more than just "offensive" or "unpleasant" (*Howard University vs. Best* 1984). Furthermore, the communication must be disclosed or published to a third person who has no legitimate interest in the matter. In *Howard University vs. Best*, the chair of the department of pharmacy practice was denied reappointment and sued the university for, among other things, defamation. Best alleged that she was defamed by reports prepared by outside consultants containing statements that she was actively opposed to, and failed to cooperate with, the present administration.

The court held that a publication is defamatory if it tends to injure the faculty member in her profession or community standing; lowers her in the estimation of the academic community; is more than unpleasant or offensive; and makes the faculty member appear odious, infamous, or ridiculous. The court held that the report was not defamatory, and even if it was, Best failed to prove that anyone received or circulated the report. As this court indicated, even if the statement has the potential to injure the faculty member's reputation, it must be "published"; that is, a third person must be made aware of the statement.

Defamation also requires that the statement be false. Therefore, opinions usually are not considered defamatory because they cannot be "false." Opinions, however, can be considered defamatory if they are based on facts that can be verified as false. This can be difficult too. In *Baker vs. Lafayette College* (1987), a faculty member in the art department, who had talked about the department chairperson's behavioral problems with certain administrators and staff members, was denied reappointment. He alleged that evaluations made by the chairperson and an outside consultant were defamatory, and a committee reviewing the matter determined that the evaluations were faulty and should be reperformed. The court indicated that for an opinion to be defamatory it must imply the existence of undisclosed defamatory facts justifying the opinion. The court held that none of the statements in the evaluation were defamatory; the reports included frank opinion void of innuendo and the information was not based upon any undisclosed facts.

Institutions and peer evaluators usually can successfully avoid liability for comments or statements made during the peer-review process under a number of theories. High-level administrators at public institutions sometimes can claim "official immunity" from tort liability (Kaplin and Lee 1995). For such immunity to apply, the individual's act must be discretionary and within his or her scope of authority. In states with such immunity, presidents, provosts, department chairs, and deans enjoy immunity if they acted in good faith — that is, without malice or ill will (see *Koerselman vs. Rhynard* 1994; *Staheli vs. Smith* 1989).

Administrators at public institutions, on the other hand, cannot escape liability for violating the civil or constitutional rights of faculty members. Section 1983 allows faculty members to sue state and local employees for violations of constitutional or civil rights. In *United Carolina Bank vs. Board of Regents of Stephen F. Austin State University* (1982), a professor denied tenure sued several administrators, claiming that the negative decision was based upon allegations he had made concerning misuse of funds. The faculty member claimed that these allegations were an exercise of his First Amendment rights. The administrators claimed immunity, arguing they did not know that their actions would violate the professor's First Amendment rights. The court rejected their arguments and held them personally liable (Kaplin and Lee).

In *Dube vs. State University of New York* (1990), also discussed in Section Three, the court also refused to grant immunity to administrators who may have violated the First Amendment rights of a faculty member. Ernest Dube, an assistant professor of African studies at SUNY Stonybrook, developed a course titled "The Politics of Race," in which he interpreted Nazism, Apartheid, and Zionism as three forms of racism. Controversy arose over the course, which was removed from the curriculum, and the institution postponed Dube's tenure review. A year later, the first-level tenure committee voted unanimously in favor of promotion and tenure, but the second-level committee voted narrowly for tenure but not promotion.

The dean of humanities and fine arts recommended against promotion and tenure, citing Dube's weak scholarship. The provost also recommended against tenure, citing the unusual vote for tenure but not promotion and Dube's meager publication record. Dube appealed to the chancellor of SUNY, who appointed a three-member committee. The committee recommended that Dube be granted tenure but released their findings to the press before the chancellor could consider the matter. A second committee was appointed, which recommended tenure but not promotion, or in the alternative, that Dube's contract be extended for another three years. The chancellor denied Dube's application for promotion and tenure. Dube sued SUNY and all of the personnel involved in the promotion and tenure process, alleging violations of Section 1983 and the First Amendment, among other issues. Although the court held that the 11th Amendment of the Constitution, which gives states immunity from lawsuits, protected SUNY, it did not protect state officials who are sued in their personal and individual capacities for violations of First Amendment rights. Accordingly, the court determined that the individual defendants in this case are not immune from liability under Section 1983 nor are they immune from liability for violations of the First and 14th amendments of the Constitution (see Bickel and Bulbin 1990).

Although individual peer reviewers may be found liable for violations of faculty members' constitutional and civil rights, courts generally will grant them a qualified privilege against defamation because the interest of peer evaluators in effectively evaluating faculty members for reappointment, promotion, or tenure is so important that some latitude should be made for mistakes. Even negative employment references and performance evaluations are privileged, therefore, if they are made in good faith and distributed only to those with a legitimate interest in them. In *Byers vs. Kolodziej* (1977), evaluators stated during the tenure-review process that "neither the quality or the quantity" of a faculty member's scholarly work justified granting him tenure. Such a statement was held privileged in the setting of faculty evaluation (Olswang and Lee 1992).

Also, in *Staheli vs. Smith* (1989), an associate professor of geology and geological engineering at the University of Mississippi sued the dean of the engineering school, who had recommended against tenure and a pay raise in a letter commenting strongly on the faculty member's performance. The faculty member sued for defamation. The court held that the dean enjoyed a qualified privilege against defamation liability when there was no proof that he intentionally stated a falsehood, acted with malice (that is, with intent to injure another person), or greatly exceeded his authority. Furthermore, the allegedly defamatory remarks were not communicated to people who did not have an interest in the matter.

A qualified privilege also has been applied even when the communication does not relate directly to the faculty member's qualifications. In *Koerselman vs. Rhynard* (1994), Rhynard, a faculty member at the music department of Sam Houston State University, was denied tenure. Koerselman, the chair of the music department, had written a letter to the dean recommending against tenure and stating that some students had complained that Rhynard had made "inappropriate comments," some with "sexual overtones." Rhynard sued Koerselman and others for defamation. The court held that the chairperson at a state university has official immunity from defamation (and other tort claims). Furthermore, defamatory communications, the court held, are privileged when made in good faith (honest or without malice) on any subject matter in which person has an interest or duty to perform.

Courts, however, will not grant an absolute privilege in a defamation lawsuit. It would be unfair to grant such a privilege because the faculty member whose reputation is injured would have no legal recourse. In *Goodman vs. Gallerano* (1985), a professor of economics sued two faculty members who stated orally and in writing that he had mismanaged funds, plagiarized research, and violated professional ethics while he was being considered for tenure at the University of Dallas. The two faculty members had filed charges of "unprofessional conduct" against Goodman, and these were forwarded to the Rank and Tenure Committee, which denied him tenure. The court held that these allegations were not absolutely privileged since to do so would unnecessarily deny innocent victims the right to seek compensation. The court indicated that these faculty members would have a qualified privilege if they acted in good faith and without malice.

This qualified privilege, therefore, can be lost if the person being accused of defamation made the statement on an improper occasion, acted in bad faith, or excessively "published" the statement (Kaplin and Lee 1995, p. 130). The institutions should inform its peer reviewers, therefore, that they should investigate the "facts" that provide the basis for the potentially defamatory statement to ensure that the statement is true or that it is reasonable to believe it to be true. Peer reviewers also should not consider innuendos nor should they communicate their findings to people who have no interest in the matter. And any opinion must be based upon disclosed and truthful information.

Institutions and peer reviewers also may avoid liability for defamation and other liability claims on the grounds that the faculty member consented to the evaluation. By agreeing to have his or her credentials evaluated for the purposes of reappointment, promotion, or tenure, a faculty member consents to others commenting on those credentials (Kaplin and Lee 1995; Olswang and Lee 1992).

Finally, if a faculty member at a public institution is denied reappointment, promotion, or tenure based upon a negative evaluation, he or she may be able to claim a "liberty interest" under the 14th Amendment, thus requiring the institution to provide him or her with due process procedures (notice and an opportunity to be heard, for example) to refute the evaluation. The statement must be such that it imposes on the faculty member a "stigma" or prevents him or her from getting other employment (*Board of Regents vs. Roth* 1972). But as the Supreme Court indicated in *Bishop vs. Wood* (1976), liberty interests are not implicated if the statements were not publicly disclosed. Faculty members at public institutions subject to sunshine laws, apparently, may be able to sustain a claim of defamation if stigmatizing or defamatory statements are contained in their personnel files, and these files are subject to public review.

The Scenario

Let us return to the hypothetical situation mentioned at the start of this section. You sought to learn how the peer-review committee voted on your promotion application, fearing gender discrimination may have occurred. Are you confident that you can obtain the information you seek? Much of your case depends upon whether you have some evidence that discrimination has occurred (comments overheard by you or others or statistical evidence, for example). It is unlikely that your institution will voluntarily inform you how particular members of the committee voted. If you have some evidence of discrimination, perhaps the institution will provide you with a redacted copy of the committee deliberations. But is a redacted copy of the committee's deliberations sufficient? What if you have reason to believe that specific members of the committee discriminated against you? If you file a claim with the EEOC, then the EEOC is likely to get the information from the institution, and if not, it is likely to convince a court to compel your institution to turn over the information.

As a result of *University of Pennsylvania vs. E.E.O.C.* (1990), the institution is not likely to prevail by claiming a common-law or academic freedom privilege. If you sue, it also is likely that you can compel the disclosure of the information. If your state's laws permit you access to this information, you can obtain it just by asking. Your state, however, may have other laws that protect the privacy of peer reviewers. If this is the case, perhaps you successfully can argue that the need to disclose potentially discriminatory information outweighs the peer reviewers' right to privacy.

Summary

Peer-review committees have great discretion in evaluating candidates for reappointment, promotion, and tenure. They may use any method of evaluating candidates as long as they do not arbitrarily or capriciously. Faculty members denied reappointment, promotion, or tenure often are left with very little understanding of the basis for the decision and without a meaningful opportunity to challenge any negative information. As a result, a faculty member or the EEOC may be able to obtain access to peer-review materials to discover proof of discrimination if either initiates a suit against an institution. Furthermore, in some states, peer evaluations generally are made available to faculty members under employee right-to-know or sunshine laws (Olswang and Lee 1992).

Despite the trend in courts of granting access to peer-review materials, they have been very deferential to the substance of peer-review decisions and have constantly refused to substitute their judgments for those of peer reviewers (Hendrickson 1991; Lee 1985). Although faculty members alleging discrimination have been given access to their personnel files and the files of other professors, courts generally have been concerned with the impact this disclosure has on the peer-review process. As a result, courts continue to search for a balance between the importance of confidentiality for the peer-review system and the need to prohibit discrimination in higher education (Hendrickson 1991).

The peer-review system likely will not suffer from disclosure of confidential peer-review materials. Peer evaluations based on sound and fair reasoning will always withstand challenges. For example, in *Bina vs. Providence College* (1994), the faculty member of Iranian descent lost his discrimination case because the tenure-committee minutes clearly showed no evidence of discrimination. Furthermore, in states in which sunshine and employee right-to-know laws include personnel files, the peer-review system does not appear to suffer.

Even though courts will compel disclosure in some situations, the decision of whether to release peer-review materials to the faculty member is one of institutional policy (Olswang and Lee 1992). Some institutions provide faculty members denied reappointment, promotion, or tenure with, at a minimum, a redacted copy of the peer-review materials, and recent data indicate that the peer-review system is not greatly affected by disclosure of peer-review materials (Olswang and Lee 1992). All institutions, however, should inform peer reviewers that confidentiality cannot be guaranteed.

Although faculty members and administrators involved in the peer-review process can be sued for defamation and other torts, they usually are protected from liability by state law or a qualified privilege. Also, most institutions have insurance covering this type of matter. Of course, peer reviewers can lose this protection if they act with malice, bad faith, or disclose the information to people with no legitimate interest in the matter. Peer reviewers, however, should understand that as long as they acted honestly and fairly and provided detailed examples for their conclusions, they are protected from liability and the integrity of the peer-review system is maintained.

RECOMMENDATIONS FOR POLICY AND PRACTICE

As we have indicated, courts provide institutions with a great deal of autonomy from judicial review in employment matters. Faculty members usually have lost their lawsuits. LaNoue and Lee pointed out that only one in five faculty member prevailed in Title VII suits (1987)*. This does not mean, of course, that faculty members will not continue to sue institutions when they are denied reappointment, promotion, or tenure, even if the decision is valid from a legal standpoint. A decline in enrollments at many colleges has led to serious staff reductions, resulting in fewer teaching positions. Given the financial expense of tenure, some institutions also are establishing tenure quotas. Lawsuits, therefore, are likely to increase.

Financial constraints and legal obligations create a need to validate criteria and procedures so that institutions can make fine distinctions between generally competent faculty members (Biernat 1987; Centra 1979). By reviewing their policies and practices to ensure that they are within legal parameters, institutions can do much to minimize lawsuits or at least to demonstrate to courts that they did not act arbitrarily.

The following suggestions are intended to minimize the risk of litigation, but they should not be read as legal advice. Each institution has its own special needs, particular legal obligations, and political climate. Each institution should consult with its attorney if it wishes to change or modify its current policies and procedures. These recommendations, however, may clarify particular concerns at some institutions, and they may provide administrators and faculty members with information that may assist them in consulting with their attorneys.

Institutions should involve legal counsel in setting policy and procedures for reappointment, promotion, and tenure decisions. Regardless of what kind of legal services institutions have (for example, in-house counsel, state attorney, or a private law firm), legal counsel performs two basic roles: treatment and preventive law. Treatment law focuses on actual challenges to the institution's policies or practices, such as when lawsuits are filed or threatened; when the institution is cited for noncompliance by a govern-

---

*This does not take into account settlements.

ment agency; or when the institution wishes to sue (Kaplin and Lee 1995). Preventive law, on the other hand, focuses on initiatives an institution should take to avoid litigation.

Preventive law should be emphasized. The attorney may help administrators and faculty members involved in reappointment, promotion, and tenure decisions by identifying the legal consequences of proposed actions, pinpointing the range of alternatives for avoiding legal problems, identifying the legal risks of each alternative, sensitizing administrators to legal issues and the importance of recognizing them early, and determining the impact of new or proposed laws, regulations, and court decisions on institutional practice (Kaplin and Lee 1995). Administrators, faculty members, and attorneys should perform legal audits periodically. These legal audits involve surveying each office and function to ensure that policies and practices comply with legal principles. Furthermore, a legal audit can serve as an early warning system that alerts administrators, faculty members, and legal counsel of potential legal problems long before they lead to litigation.

The reappointment, promotion, and tenure policies and procedures should be explicit, unambiguous, and consistent. Administrators should exercise great care in drafting employment contracts and institutional policies because courts will first look to the actual language or words of these sources to determine the rights and responsibilities of both parties. All terms should be defined and written in a manner that is easy to understand. Institutions should ensure that all employees receive a copy of the policy, and administrators should be trained to administer the policies appropriately. All employment applications, contracts, handbooks, policies, procedures, guidelines, and work rules should be periodically reviewed to ensure that they are consistent with each other and clearly delineate each party's rights and responsibilities. Carelessly drafted policies and procedures lead to confusion and litigation. Furthermore, courts would be forced to resort to informal sources (institutional practices and verbal assurances of key administrators, for example) to resolve the issue.

Institutions should pay careful attention to those practices or customs that are not specifically addressed in

the institutions' written policies. Courts have looked to these informal practices when the language of a contract is ambiguous or inconsistent. Some practices have evolved despite written policies. Institutions should put in writing those practices that are to be part of the faculty contract of employment and eliminate or cease those that are not. Once put in writing, it is extremely important for administrators and faculty members to adhere to the written policies or they will not be able to justify any decisions based upon those policies.

Institutional officers and key administrators should be informed that their actions and words can bind the institutions to a contract. Presidents, vice presidents, deans, and department heads should be informed that their actions and oral assurances or promises can create contractual rights for faculty members, although oral modifications of written contracts generally are held to be invalid and unenforceable. Nevertheless, some courts have upheld such contracts in a few instances in which the actions of administrators clearly warranted such findings. Institutions should clearly and explicitly state which officer or administrator may bind the institution to an employment contract. For example, the institution may indicate in the contract or the faculty handbook that only the president may bind the institution to an oral contract. This kind of statement not only protects the institution but faculty members are put on notice that they may not rely upon the assurances of those who cannot keep their promises.

Policies should indicate clearly and explicitly how reappointment, promotion, or tenure is to be acquired. Policies that are silent or unclear as to how tenure is acquired may result in a judicial finding of tenure by default or de facto tenure. Clear and explicit policies protect the institution's right to reward those faculty members deemed to have earned it, and faculty members are clearly informed of the criteria and procedures for the acquisition of promotion or tenure. Of course, some institutions have automatic reappointment, promotion, and tenure policies, and they may not want to change their policies. All institutions, however, should consider relevant state laws, collective-bargaining agreements, and the impact on faculty recruitment and

Policies that are silent or unclear as to how tenure is acquired may result in a judicial finding of tenure by default or de facto tenure.

morale prior to initiating any kind of significant change in their policies.

All units in the institution should be governed by a single reappointment, promotion, and tenure policy. Colleges or universities should adopt a single policy that specifies the minimum eligibility requirements for reappointment, promotion, and tenure. This policy also should govern the process, procedures, and timing of the decisions as well as any notification and appeals guidelines. This way, all faculty members are treated in a consistent manner, regardless of the department to which they belong. At large university systems, a single policy governing these employment decisions may seem difficult, especially when the individual colleges, schools, and departments all have different standards (McKee 1980). But inconsistency promotes litigation. The single policy is not meant to take away discretion but to ensure fairness for all faculty members. Although such a policy would prescribe minimum eligibility requirements (excellence in teaching, research, and service, for example), it still should allow each department or discipline to determine whether and how faculty members qualify for reappointment, promotion, or tenure.

The criteria for reappointment, promotion, or tenure should be specific enough to provide guidance to the faculty member. Institutions enjoy extensive deference from the courts in determining the criteria for employment decisions. Many institutions also provide little concrete information about its criteria and how faculty members satisfy them. Ambiguous criteria lead to confusion, uncertainty, and, ultimately, litigation. The criteria should be specific enough to provide faculty members with guidance as to what is expected of them and flexible enough to allow administrators and peer-review committees to consider the faculty members' total accomplishments. Institutions, for example, may inform faculty members that "service" must include departmental and institutionwide committees. Institutions also may base reappointment, promotion, or tenure on such considerations as the priorities of the institution, new and developing disciplines, interdisciplinary and collaborative work, and special assignments (see Diamond

1994). Faculty members, however, should be made aware of the specific criteria used by the institution.

Faculty members should be provided with as much information as possible as they prepare for their reappointment, promotion, or tenure review. The more information the candidate receives as he or she prepares for review, the easier the process will be for the candidate, the committee, administrators, and the institution. Ideally, faculty members should receive information in four areas: the type of documentation expected from them; the specific steps that will be followed by the committee; the criteria that will be used to assess the quality of the materials that are provided; and how the various activities of the faculty member will be weighed (Diamond 1994).

Faculty members should be entitled to procedural safeguards before they are released from their contracts. Although the Constitution does not require colleges and universities to provide untenured faculty members with minimal due process requirements, most institutions do provide them. This is sound practice, as it ensures that faculty members are treated fairly and insulates the institutions from allegations of arbitrariness. Institutions should provide faculty members with adequate reasons for the negative decision and appropriate notice, and faculty members should be entitled to an internal grievance mechanism. The AAUP's Standards for Notice of Nonreappointment (AAUP 1990) requires 12 months' notice in advance of dismissal for a faculty member employed for more than two years. This practice provides faculty members with time to relocate or to seek reconsideration of a negative decision before their existing appointments have expired (Brown and Kurland 1993). Such procedural safeguards allow institutions to avoid mistakes or rectify them, protects the faculty members' academic freedom and other rights, and decreases the probability of lawsuits. If a lawsuit occurs — and some will — courts will look favorably upon institutions that have these safeguards.

Institutions should provide orientation and career development for new faculty members. Orientation and career development for new faculty members helps them understand and deal with institutional expectations and helps to ensure their success (Boice 1992). Furthermore, by providing these services, institutions show faculty members that they want them to succeed. Senior faculty members should be encouraged to become mentors for young faculty members, giving them advice, collaborating with them on projects, and evaluating their performances (Boice 1992; Leap 1993). Of course, faculty members who become mentors should be rewarded by the institutions.

Institutions should develop a process of annually evaluating faculty members. Faculty members should be evaluated before the tenure decision is made. An annual performance evaluation would be useful for everyone involved. The institution benefits from alerting faculty members to potential problems, and it develops a written record should litigation later arise. The faculty member benefits because he or she is alerted to potential problems and has an opportunity to improve. These evaluations should be meaningful and constructive, accurate and timely, relevant and candid and provided in both formative and summative settings; otherwise, no one benefits. The institution should use multiple methods of evaluation such as teaching portfolios, student evaluations, and peer evaluations (Centra 1993). The information used in these evaluations also should be job-related and nondiscriminatory.

The faculty member should be apprised of any performance problem with enough time to improve. The faculty member should not be surprised by his or her colleagues' negative evaluation at the time the tenure decision is made. Such a surprise leads to anger and is unfair. If the faculty member is alerted of any performance problem before the summative evaluation is made, he or she has the opportunity to improve. At the very least, the faculty member is put on notice that his or her performance is inadequate. This practice should be intended to improve faculty performance and to assist in making reappointment, promotion, or tenure decisions, but it also provides a written documentation of the problem and the notice of it to the faculty member should litigation arise.

Faculty members should have the opportunity to review, comment upon, and sign the performance evaluation. In this way, if the faculty member has any objections, he or she can state them at that time. The institution then may conduct an immediate investigation which would promote the resolution of the matter within its borders (Biernat 1987). Of course, any information that may hurt the faculty member's reputation should be investigated. All facts forming the basis of any allegation must be true; innuendos should not form the basis of any allegations. And the information should not be released to noninterested parties.

Faculty members denied reappointment, promotion, or tenure should be provided with, at the very least, a redacted copy of their performance evaluations and peer-review material upon request. Everyone involved in the faculty-evaluation process should understand that peer-review materials may be subject to disclosure, especially in employment-discrimination cases. These materials, therefore, should be prepared with care. Although peer-review materials need not be disclosed unless a lawsuit or EEOC claim is initiated, institutions should have internal policies governing the disclosure of peer-review materials, personnel records, or performance evaluations. Institutions should consider releasing these materials upon request, at least in redacted form, to a faculty member subjected to a negative employment decision.

The number of people with access to this information should be limited, of course. But providing this information to the faculty member may prevent extensive litigation, especially if the faculty member does not have a legitimate claim. Colleges and universities should consider having a "gatekeeper" who is trained in the fundamentals of state and federal law as well as institutional policies (Cunningham, Leeson, and Stadler 1988). This gatekeeper is responsible for these types of requests and may provide the faculty members with a comprehensive summary of a decision and, if there is enough evidence to indicate that the decision may have been motivated by illegal factors, more information may be released to the faculty member. Faculty members also should have access to their personnel files and redacted copies of others' files if necessary when they file an internal grievance.

Institutions should commit themselves to ending discrimination and take whatever steps are necessary to achieve this end. The commitment to end discrimination may lead to a complete restructuring of the decision-making process (Biernat 1987). But colleges and universities must be able to defend their practices, and the best defense is to eliminate discrimination. Toward this end, an institution may establish educational programs and sensitivity training and prohibit openly biased people from participating in reappointment, promotion, and tenure decisions. Establishing mentoring programs for women and people of color also will assist these faculty members to succeed.

Institutions should be conscious of the important legal, political, and social interests associated with affirmative action. The conflict between institutional and individual rights is most greatly illustrated in affirmative-action cases. The institution's right to use race or gender, not to harm women or people of color but to assist them, appears to have recently given way to the individual rights of faculty members who are not part of any protected groups. Affirmative-action programs have been justified on important institutional and societal interests such as to remedy the effects of past discrimination and to increase diversity. These justifications do not appear to be sufficient today.

Although some affirmative-action plans are currently legal, the viability of these programs is in a state of flux in today's political and social climate. Arguably, without affirmative action women and people of color may be subject to discrimination, leading to a violation of their individual rights. So, the battles about affirmative action may involve determining *whose* individual rights are more prominent. Regardless of how this plays out in the political, social, and judicial arenas, the institutions likely will be in the difficult position of struggling with very important interests: the need to repay certain groups of people for previous discrimination and to increase the diversity in its faculty ranks and the need to judge faculty members solely on the quality of their performance.

Individuals involved in the evaluation or review process must be made aware of the fundamentals of employment-discrimination law. Faculty members, administrators, and even students involved in the reappointment, promotion, or tenure process should understand the legal principles of employment discrimination. This is not to tie their hands or take away their discretion but to make them aware of potentially illegal practices.

Institutions should establish grievance procedures that are easy to use. Most institutions have a grievance process that permits faculty members to challenge negative employment decisions. Grievance procedures should be known and available to all faculty members. These procedures should be easy to use and provide faculty members with a fair opportunity to be heard. Furthermore, the decisions of grievance committees should be consistent and fair.

Institutions should consider adopting binding arbitration or other methods of dispute resolution. Arbitration is common in collective-bargaining agreements. And as some of the cases indicate, arbitration can be useful in preventing protracted litigation. This type of nonjudicial resolution may be less adversarial than litigation and may minimize the legal, financial, and emotional expenses involved in litigation. Arbitration, however, also can be burdensome and complicated. As with grievance procedures, arbitration and dispute-resolution policies and procedures also should be easy to use.

Some Final Words

Faculty members do not always prevail in lawsuits against institutions because of a legitimate legal claim but because judges or juries believe they were treated unfairly (Olswang 1992). To ensure fairness, institutions should evaluate faculty members realistically and accurately. They should discuss any problem or potential problems directly with the faculty member, and these discussions should be completely and accurately documented. Faculty members should receive constructive criticism and be permitted to improve prior to being discharged, and they should be warned that if they do not improve they may be released (Olswang 1992). If a faculty member must be released from his or her contract, an institution should be prepared to show that there are good reasons for the decision (inadequate teaching or scholarship, for example), and these reasons must be substantiated with credible evidence. This is not only sound practice from a legal standpoint, but it also is fair.

LIST OF CASES

AAUP vs. Bloomfield College, 322 A.2d 846 (Ch. Divs. 1974).

Adarand Constructors, Inc. vs. Pena, 115 S. Ct. 2097 (1995).

Ahmadieh, et al. vs. State Board of Agriculture, 767 P.2d 746 (Col. Ct. of Appeals 1988).

Association of New Jersey State College Faculties vs. Dungan, 316 A.2d 425 (1974).

Baker vs. Lafayette College, 504 A.2d 247 (Pa. Super. Ct. 1986).

Baker vs. Lafayette College, 532 A.2d 399 (Pa. 1987).

Beckwith vs. Rhode Island School of Design, 404 A.2d 480 (R.I. 1979).

Bina vs. Providence College, 844 F. Supp. 77 (D.R.I. 1994).

Bishop vs. Wood, 426 U.S. 341 (1976).

Board of Regents of State Colleges vs. Roth, 408 U.S. 564 (1972).

Board of Trustees vs. Superior Court, 119 Cal. App. 3d 516 (1981), cert. denied, *Doug vs. Board of Trustees*, 484 U.S. 1019 (1988).

Bradford College, 261 N.L.R.B. 565 (1982).

Brown vs. Board of Education of Topeka, 347 U.S. 483 (1954).

Brown vs. Trustees of Boston University, 891 F.2d 337 (1st Cir. 1989).

Bruno vs. Detroit Institute of Technology, 215 N.W.2d 745 (1974).

Byers vs. Kolodziej, 363 N.E.2d 628 (Ill. App. Ct. 1977).

Chung vs. Park, 514 F.2d 382 (3d Cir. 1975).

City of Richmond vs. J. A. Croson Co., 488 U.S. 469 (1989).

Clark vs. Claremont University Center, 8 Cal. Rptr. 2d 151 (Cal. App. 2 Dist. 1992).

Coe vs. Board of Regents of University of Wisconsin, 409 N.W.2d 166 (Wis. App. 1987).

Colburn vs. Trustees of Indiana University, 739 F. Supp. 1268 (S.D. Ind. 1990).

Cooper vs. Ross, 472 F. Supp. 802 (E.D. Ark. 1979).

Craig vs. Alabama State University, 451 F. Supp. 1207 (M.D. Ala. 1978).

C.W. Post Center of Long Island University, 189 N.L.R.B. 904 (1971).

Desimone vs. Skidmore College, 517 N.Y.S.2d 880 (Sup. Ct. 1987).

Dixon vs. Rutgers, 521 A.2d 1315 (N.J. Super. A.D. 1987).

Dube vs. State University of New York, 900 F.2d 587 (2d Cir. 1990).

Dusquesne University, 261 N.L.R.B. 587 (1982).

E.E.O.C. vs. Catholic University of America, 856 F. Supp. 1 (D.D.C. 1994).

E.E.O.C. vs. Franklin & Marshall College, 775 F.2d 110 (3d Cir. 1985).

E.E.O.C. vs. University of Notre Dame Du Lac, 715 F.2d 331 (7th Cir. 1983).

Enright vs. California State University, 57 Fair Empl. Prac. Cases 56 (E.D. Cal. 1989).

Faculty of the City University of New York Law School at Queens College vs. Murphy, 539 N.Y.S.2d 367 (A.D. 1 Department. 1989).

Fisher vs. Asheville-Buncombe Technical College, 857 F. Supp. 465 (W.D.N.C. 1993).

Ford vs. Nicks, 866 F.2d 865 (6th Cir. 1989).

Ganguli vs. University of Minnesota, 512 N.W.2d 918 (Minn. Ct. App. 1994).

Goodman vs. Board of Trustees of Community College District 525, 511 F. Supp. 602 (N.D. Ill. 1981).

Goodman vs. Gallerano, 695 S.W.2d 286 (Tex. App. 5 Dist. 1985).

Goodship vs. University of Richmond, 860 F. Supp. 1110 (E.D.Va. 1994).

Goss vs. San Jacinto Junior College, 588 F.2d 96 (5th Cir. 1979).

Gray vs. Board of Higher Education, City of New York, 692 F.2d 901 (2d Cir. 1982).

Greene vs. Howard University, 412 F.2d 1128 (D.C. Cir. 1969).

Griggs vs. Duke Power Co., 401 U.S. 424 (1971).

Gutzwiller vs. Fenik, 860 F.2d 1317 (6th Cir. 1988).

Hackel vs. Vermont State Colleges, 438 A.2d 1119 (Vt. 1981).

Halpin vs. LaSalle University, 639 A.2d 37 (Pa. Super. Ct. 1994).

Hander vs. San Jacinto Junior College, 519 F.2d 273 (5th Cir. 1975).

Hill vs. Talledega College, 502 So. 2d 735 (Ala. 1987).

Honore vs. Douglas, 833 F.2d 565 (5th Cir. 1987).

Howard University vs. Best, 484 A.2d 958 (D.C. App. 1984).

In Re Dinnan, 661 F.2d 426 (5th Cir. 1981), *cert. denied*, 457 U.S. 1106 (1982).

International Association of Firefighters vs. City of Cleveland, 106 S. Ct. 3063 (1986).

Ithaca College, 261 N.L.R.B. 577 (1982).

J. Carpenter vs. Board of Regents, University of Wisconsin System, 728 F.2d 911 (7th Cir. 1984).

Jackson vs. Harvard University, 111 F.R.D. 472 (D. Mass. 1986).

Jackson vs. Harvard University, 900 F.2d 464 (1st Cir. 1990).

Jeffries vs. Harleston, 828 F. Supp. 1066 (S.D.N.Y. 1993), *affirmed*, 21 F.2d 1238 (2nd Cir. 1994), *reversed and remanded*, 115 S.Ct. 502 (1995), *reconsidered*, 52 F.3d 9 (2nd Cir. 1995), *cert. denied*, 115 S. Ct. 1265 (1995).

Jimenez vs. Almodovar, 650 F.2d 363 (1st Cir. 1981).

Johnson vs. Transportation Agency, Santa Clara County, 480 U.S. 616 (1987).

Jones vs. University of Central Oklahoma, 13 F.3d 361 (10th Cir. 1993).

Kahn vs. Superior Court of the County of Santa Clara, 233 Cal. Rptr. 662 (1987).

Keyishian vs. Board of Regents, 365 U.S. 589 (1967).

King vs. Board of Regents of University of Wisconsin System, 898 F.2d 533 (7th Cir. 1990).

King vs. University of Minnesota, 774 F.2d 224 (8th Cir. 1985).

Knowles vs. Unity College, 429 A.2d 220 (Me. 1981).

Koerselman vs. Rhynard, 875 S.W.2d 347 (Tex. App. — Corpus Christi 1994).

Korbin vs. University of Minnesota, 34 F.3d 698 (8th Cir. 1994).

Korf vs. Ball State University, 726 F.2d 1222 (7th Cir. 1984).

Krotkoff vs. Goucher College, 585 F.2d 675 (4th Cir. 1978).

Kunda vs. Muhlenberg College, 621 F.2d 532 (3d Cir. 1980).

Lafayette College vs. Comm. of Pennsylvania, Department of Labor and Industry, Bureau of Labor Standards, 546 A.2d 126 (Pa. Cmmwlth. 1988).

Levi vs. University of Texas at San Antonio, 840 F.2d 277 (5th Cir. 1988).

Levin vs. Harleston, 770 F. Supp. 895 (S.D.N.Y. 1991).

Levin vs. Harleston, 966 F.2d 85 (2d Cir. 1992).

Lewis University, 265 N.L.R.B. No. 157 (1982).

Lewis vs. Loyola University of Chicago, 500 N.E.2d 47 (Ill. App. 1 Dist. 1986).

Local 28 of Sheet Metal Workers' International Association vs. E.E.O.C., 106 S. Ct. 3019 (1986).

Loretto Heights College vs. N.L.R.B., 742 F.2d 1245 (10th Cir. 1984).

Lovelace vs. Southeastern Massachusetts University, 793 F.2d 419 (1st Cir. 1986).

Marwil vs. Baker, 499 F. Supp. 560 (E.D. Mich. 1980).

McDonnell Douglas Corp. vs. Green, 411 U.S. 792 (1973).

Meyer vs. Nebraska, 262 U.S. 390 (1923).

Moche vs. City University of New York, 781 F. Supp. 160 (E.D.N.Y. 1992).

Muskovitz vs. Lubbers, 452 N.W.2d 854 (Mich. Ct. App. 1990).

N.L.R.B. vs. Catholic Bishop of Chicago, 440 UNITED STATES 490 (1979).

N.L.R.B. vs. Florida Memorial College, 820 F.2d 1182 (11th Cir. 1987).

N.L.R.B. vs. Stephens Institute, 620 F.2d 720 (9th Cir. 1980).

N.L.R.B. vs. Yeshiva University, 100 S. Ct. 856 (1980).

Neiman vs. Kingsborough Community College, 536 N.Y.S.2d 843 (A.D. 2 Department. 1989).

Omlor vs. Cleveland State University, 543 N.E.2d 1238 (Ohio 1989).

Olson vs. Idaho State University, 868 P.2d 505 (Idaho Ct. App. 1994).

Orbovich vs. Macalester College, 119 F.R.D. 411 (D. Minn. 1988).

Palmer vs. District Board of Trustees of St. Petersburg Junior College, 748 F.2d 595 (11th Cir. 1984).

Parate vs. Isibor, 868 F.2d 821 (6th Cir. 1989).

Pennsylvania State University vs. Commonwealth of Pennsylvania, Department of Labor and Industry, Bureau of Labor Standards, 536 A.2d 852 (Pa. Cmmwlth. 1988).

Perry vs. Sindermann, 408 U.S. 593 (1972).

Pickering vs. Board of Education, 391 US 563 (1968).

Pime vs. Loyola University of Chicago, 803 F.2d 351 (7th Cir. 1986).

Podberesky vs. Kirwan, 38 F.2d 147 (4th Cir. 1995), cert. denied, 115 S. Ct. 2001 (1995).

Rajender vs. University of Minnesota, 546 F. Supp. 158 (D. Minn. 1982), 563 F. Supp. 401 (D. Minn. 1983).

Regents of the University of Michigan vs. Ewing, 474 U.S. 214 (1985).

Riggin vs. Board of Trustees of Ball State University, 489 N.E. 2d 616 (Ind. App. 1986).

Romer vs. Hobart and William Smith Colleges, 842 F. Supp. 703 (W.D.N.Y. 1994).

Roos vs. Smith, 837 F. Supp. 803 (S.D. Miss. 1993).

Scelsa vs. City University of New York, 806 F. Supp. 1126 (S.D.N.Y. 1992).

Scharf vs. Regents of the University of California, 286 Cal. Rptr. 227 (Cal.App.1Dist. 1991).

Scott vs. University of Delaware, 455 F. Supp. 1102 (D. Del. 1978).

Snitow vs. Rutgers University, 510 A.2d 1118 (N.J. 1986).

Sola vs. Lafayette College, 804 F.2d 40 (3d Cir. 1986).

Soni vs. Board of Trustees of the University of Tennessee, 513 F.2d 347 (6th Cir. 1975).

Staheli vs. Smith, 548 S.2d 1299 (Miss. 1989).

State Ex. Rel. James vs. Ohio State University, 637 N.E.2d 911 (Ohio 1994).

Sunshine vs. Long Island University, 862 F. Supp. 26 (E.D.N.Y. 1994).

Sweezy vs. New Hampshire, 354 US 234 (1957).

Thiel College, 261 N.L.R.B. 580 (1982).

Trister vs. University of Mississippi, 420 F.2d 499 (5th Cir. 1969).

United Carolina Bank vs. Board of Regents of Stephen F. Austin State University, 665 F.2d 553 (5th Cir. 1982).

United States vs. Paradise, 480 U.S. 149 (1987).

University of California Regents vs. Bakke, 438 U.S. 265 (1978).

University of Pennsylvania vs. E.E.O.C., 100 S.Ct. 577 (1990).

University of Pittsburgh, Case No. PERA-R-84-53-W, 25 (1987), rev'd, 21 Pa. Publ. Employee Rpts. 203 (1990).

Valentine vs. Smith, 654 F.2d 503 (8th Cir. 1981).

Washington vs. Davis, 426 U.S. 229 (1976).

Waters vs. Churchill, 114 S. Ct. 1878 (1994).

Watson vs. Fort Worth Bank & Trust, 487 UNITED STATES 977 (1988).

Weber vs. Kaiser Aluminum Co., 443 U.S. 193 (1979).

Whiting vs. Jackson State University, 616 F.2d 166 (5th Cir. 1980).

Wirsing vs. Board of Regents of the University of Colorado, 739 F. Supp. 551 (D. Colo. 1990), *affirmed without opin.*, 945 F.2d 412 (10th Cir. 1991).

Wygant vs. Jackson Board of Education, 106 S. Ct. 1842 (1986).

REFERENCES

"AAUP Re-Endorses Affirmative Action." March/April 1995. *Academe* 82(2): 6.

Academe. July/August 1992. Access to faculty personnel files: 24-29.

Aguirre Jr., A., A. Hernandez, and R. Martinez. 1995. "Perceptions of the Workplace: Focus on Minority Women Faculty." *Initiatives* 56(3): 41-50.

American Association of University Professors. 1990. The 1940 Statement of Principles on Academic Freedom and Tenure. In *Policy Documents & Reports* ("The AAUP Red Book"). Washington, D.C.: American Association of University Professors.

Anderson, T. 1988. "Black Encounter of Racism and Elitism in White Academe: A Critique of the System." *Journal of Black Studies* 18(3): 259-72.

Baglione, F.M. 1987. "Title VII and the Tenure Decision: The Need for a Qualified Academic Freedom Privilege Protecting Confidential Peer Review Materials in University Employment Discrimination Cases." *Suffolk University Law Review* 21: 691-721.

Banks, W.M. 1984. "Afro-American Scholars in the University: Roles and Conflicts." *American Behavioral Scientist* 27(3): 325-38.

Barrow, C.L.H. 1990. "Academic Freedom and the University Title VII Suit After *University of Pennsylvania vs. EEOC* and *Brown vs. Trustees of Boston University.*" *Vanderbilt Law Review* 43: 1,571-06.

Bednash, G. 1991. "Tenure Review: Process and Outcomes." *Review of Higher Education* 15(1): 47-63.

Bickel, R.D., and J.B. Bulbin, eds. July 1990. *The College Administrator and the Courts.* College Administration Publications, Inc.

Biernat, L. 1987. "Subjective Criteria in Faculty Employment Decisions Under Title VII: A Camouflage for Discrimination and Sexual Harassment." *University of California, Davis, Law Review* 20: 501-49.

Black's Law Dictionary. 1991. 6th ed. St. Paul, Minn.: West Publishing Co.

Blackwell, J.E. 1988. "Faculty Issues: The Impact on Minorities." *The Review of Higher Education* 11(4): 417-34.

Boice, R. 1992. *The New Faculty Member: Supporting and Fostering Professional Development.* San Francisco: Jossey-Bass.

Brookes, M.C.T., K.L. German. 1983. *Meeting the Challenges: Developing Faculty Careers.* ASHE-ERIC Higher Education Report No. 3. Washington, D.C.: Association for the Study of Higher Education. ED 232 516. 54 pp. MF-01; PC-03.

Brown, R.S., and J.E. Kurland. 1993. "Academic Tenure and Academic Freedom." In *Freedom and Tenure in the Academy*, edited by W.W. Van Alstyne. Durham, N.C.: Duke University Press.

Cahn, S.M., ed. 1993. *Affirmative Action and the University: A Philosophical Inquiry*. Philadelphia: Temple University Press.

Centra, J.A. 1979. *Determining Faculty Effectiveness: Assessing Teaching, Research, and Service for Personnel Decisions and Improvement*. San Francisco: Jossey-Bass.

———. 1993. *Reflective Faculty Evaluation: Enhancing Teaching and Determining Faculty Effectiveness*. San Francisco: Jossey-Bass.

Chait, R.P., and A.T. Ford. 1982. *Beyond Traditional Tenure: A Guide to Sound Policies and Practices*. San Francisco: Jossey-Bass.

Chan, S., and L. Wang. 1991. "Racism and the Model Minority: Asian-Americans in Higher Education." In *The Racial Crisis in American Higher Education*, edited by P.G. Altbach and K. Lomotey. Albany: State University of New York Press.

Chronicle of Higher Education . Feb. 3, 1995. "Credentials on Trial." A14+.

———. March 10, 1995. "Scheduling Motherhood." A14-15.

———. March 31, 1995. "Tenure Reexamined." A17-18.

———. April 28, 1995. "Affirmative Action on the Line." A12-33.

———. June 23, 1995. "Blow to Affirmative Action." A21-23.

———. Aug. 4, 1995. "Affirmative-Action Aftermath." A18+.

———. Sept. 1, 1995. Almanac Issue.

———. Sept. 8, 1995. "U. of Mass. Trustees Reject Tenure for Three Professors." A27.

Clague, M.W. 1987. "The Affirmative Action Showdown of 1986: Implications for Higher Education." *Journal of College and University Law* 14(2): 171-257.

Coates, K. June 23, 1995. "It Is Time to Create an Open System of Peer review." *Chronicle of Higher Education*: A40.

Commission on Academic Tenure in Higher Education. 1973. *Faculty Tenure: A Report and Recommendations by the Commission on Academic Tenure in Higher Education*. San Francisco: Jossey-Bass.

Cotter, W.R. January/February 1996. "Why Tenure Works." *Academe* 82: 26-9.

Cunningham, M.P., T.A. Leeson, and J.R. Stadler. 1988. *"Kahn vs. Superior Court of the County of Santa Clara:* The Right of Privacy and the Academic Freedom Privilege With Respect to Confidential Peer Review Materials." *Journal of College and University Law* 15(1): 73-85.

DeLano, M. 1987. "Discovery in University Employment

Discrimination Suits: Should Peer Review Materials Be Privileged?" *Journal of College and University Law* 14(1): 121-51.

Diamond, R.M. 1994. *Serving on Promotion and Tenure Committees: A Faculty Guide*. Bolton, Mass.: Anker Publishing Co., Inc.

Exum, W.H., R.J. Menges, B. Watkins, and P. Berglund. 1984. "Making It at the Top: Women and Minority Faculty in the Academic Labor Market." *American Behavioral Scientist* 27(3): 301-23.

Francis, L.P. 1993. "In Defense of Affirmative Action." In *Affirmative Action and the University: A Philosophical Inquiry*, edited by S.M. Cahn. Philadelphia: Temple University Press.

Franke, A.H. March/April 1995. "Tenure and the Faculty Pocketbook. *Academe*: 108.

Frost, L.E. 1991. "Shifting Meanings of Academic Freedom: An Analysis of *University of Pennsylvania vs. E.E.O.C.*" *Journal of College and University Law* 17(3): 329-50.

Gappa, J.M. 1984. *Part-Time Faculty: Higher Education at a Crossroads*. ASHE-ERIC Higher Education Report No. 3. Washington, D.C.: Association for the Study of Higher Education. ED 251 058. 129 pp. MC-01; PC-06.

Gappa, J.M., and D.W. Leslie. 1993. *The Invisible Faculty: Improving the Status of Part-Timers in Higher Education*. San Francisco: Jossey-Bass.

Gillmore, G.M. 1983. "Student Ratings as a Factor in Faculty Employment and Periodic Review." *Journal of College and University Law* 10(4): 557-76.

Hendrickson, R.M. 1991. *The Colleges, Their Constituencies, and the Courts*. Topeka, Kan.: National Organization on Legal Problems of Education.

Hendrickson, R.M., and B.A. Lee. 1983. *Academic Employment and Retrenchment: Judicial Review and Administrative Action*. ASHE-ERIC Higher Education Report No. 8. Washington, D.C.: Association for the Study of Higher Education. ED 240 972. 133 pp. MF-01; PC-06.

Hill, W.A. 1992. "Americans With Disabilities Act of 1990: Significant Overlap with Section 504 for Colleges and Universities." *Journal of College and University Law* 18(3): 389-417.

Hustoles, T.P. 1983. "Faculty and Staff Dismissals: Developing Contract and Tort Theories." *Journal of Higher Education* 10(4): 479-94.

———. October 1992. "Introduction to Tenure, Due Process, Just Cause, Developing Tort and Contract Theories, Privacy Rights, Faculty Evaluation, and Collective Bargaining." Paper presented at the Second Annual Conference on Legal Issues in Higher

Education, Burlington, Vt.

Johnson, A.B. 1981. "The Problems of Contraction: Legal Considerations in University Retrenchment." *Journal of College and University Law* 10(3): 269-324.

Johnsrud, L.K. 1993. "Women and Minority Faculty Experiences: Defining and Responding to Diverse Realities." *New Directions for Teaching and Learning* 53 (Spring 1993).

Johnsrud, L.K., and C.D. Des Jarlais. 1994. "Barriers to Tenure for Women and Minorities." *The Review of Higher Education* 17(4): 335-53.

Kaplin, W.A. 1985. *The Law of Higher Education: A Comprehensive Guide to Legal Implications of Administrative Decision Making.* 2nd ed. San Francisco: Jossey-Bass.

Kaplin, W.A., and B.A. Lee. 1990. *The Law of Higher Education: 1985-1990 Update.* National Association of College and University Attorneys.

————. 1995. *The Law of Higher Education: A Comprehensive Guide to Legal Implications of Administrative Decision Making.* 3d ed. San Francisco: Jossey-Bass.

Kogan, M., I. Moses, and E. El-Khawas. 1994. *Staffing Higher Education: Meeting New Challenges.* Higher Education Policy Series No. 27. Bristol, Pa.: Jessica Kingsley Publishers.

LaNoue, G.R., and B.A. Lee. 1987. *Academics in Court: The Consequences of Faculty Discrimination Litigation.* Ann Arbor: The University of Michigan Press.

Leap, T.L. 1993. *Tenure, Discrimination, and the Courts.* Ithaca, N.Y.: ILR Press.

Lee, B.A. 1985. "Federal Court Involvement in Academic Personnel Decisions: Impact on Peer Review." *Journal of Higher Education* 56(1): 38-54.

————. 1995. Review of the book *Tenure, Discrimination, and the Courts. Journal of Higher Education* 66(1): 115-17.

Lee, B.A., and J.P. Begin. 1984. "Criteria for Evaluating the Managerial Status of College Faculty: Applications of *Yeshiva University* by the NLRB." *Journal of College and University Law* 10(4): 515-39.

Markie, P.J. 1993. "Affirmative Action and the Awarding of Tenure." In *Affirmative Action and the University: A Philosophical Inquiry,* edited by S.M. Cahn. Philadelphia: Temple University Press.

McKee, P.W. 1980. "Tenure by Default: The Nonformal Acquisition of Academic Tenure." *Journal of College and University Law* 7(1-2): 31-56.

Menges, R.J., and W.H. Exum. 1983. "Barriers to the Progress of Women and Minority Faculty." *Journal of Higher Education* 54(2): 123-44.

Metzger, W.P. 1973. "Academic Tenure in America: A Historical Essay." In *Faculty Tenure: A Report and Recommendations by the Commission on Academic Tenure in Higher Education.* San Francisco: Jossey-Bass.

———. 1993a. "The 1940 Statement of Principles on Academic Freedom and Tenure." In *Freedom and Tenure in the Academy,* edited by W.W. Van Alstyne. Durham, N.C.: Duke University Press.

———. 1993b. "Professional and Legal Limits to Academic Freedom." *Journal of College and University Law* 20(1): 1-14.

Mickelson, R.A., and M.L. Oliver. 1991. "Making the Short List: Black Candidates and the Faculty Recruitment Process." In *The Racial Crisis in American Higher Education,* edited by P.A. Altbach and K. Lomotey. Albany: State University of New York Press.

Moll, J.H. February 1992. "Dismissal of Tenured Faculty for Incompetence, Neglect of Duty, or Unprofessional Conduct: A Discussion of *Korf vs. Ball State University* and *Riggin vs. Ball State University.* Paper presented at the Thirteenth Annual National Conference on Law and Higher Education, Clearwater Beach, Fla.

Moody Sr., C.D. 1988. "Strategies for Improving the Representation of Minority Faculty in Research Universities." *Peabody Journal of Education* 66(1): 77-90.

Mortimer, K.P., M. Bagshaw, and A.T. Masland. 1985. *Flexibility in Academic Staffing: Effective Policies and Practices.* ASHE-ERIC Higher Education Report No. 1. Washington, D.C.: Association for the Study of Higher Education. ED 260 675. 121 pp. MF-01; PC-05.

Nagle, P. 1994. "*Yeshiva*'s Impact on Collective Bargaining in Public-Sector Higher Education." *Journal of College and University Law* 20(3): 383-403.

Olivas, MA. 1989. *The Law and Higher Education: Cases and Materials on Colleges in Court.* Durham, N.C.: Carolina Academic Press.

Olswang, S.G. 1982. "Planning the Unthinkable: Issues in Institutional Reorganization and Faculty Reductions." *Journal of College and University Law* 9(4): 431-49.

———. 1988. "Union Security Provisions, Academic Freedom and Tenure: The Implications of *Chicago Teachers Union vs. Hudson.*" *Journal of College and University Law* 14(4): 539-60.

———. February 1992. "Economic Crisis: Reduction in Force." Paper presented at the Thirteenth Annual National Conference on Law and Higher Education, Clearwater Beach, Fla.

Olswang, S.G., and J.I. Fantel. 1980. "Tenure and Periodic Performance Review: Compatible Legal and Administrative

Principles." *Journal of College and University Law* 7(1-2): 1-30.

Olswang, S.G., and B.A. Lee. 1984. *Faculty Freedoms and Institutional Accountability: Interactions and Conflicts.* ASHE-ERIC Higher Education Report No. 5. Washington, D.C.: Association for the Study of Higher Education. ED 252 170. 90 pp. MF-01; PC-04.

———. February 1992. "Peer Review in the Sunshine: Legal and Practical Issues." Paper presented at the Thirteenth Annual National Conference on Law and Higher Education, Clearwater Beach, Fla.

Partain, J.J. 1987. "A Qualified Academic Freedom Privilege in Employment Litigation: Protecting Higher Education or Shielding Discrimination?" *Vanderbilt Law Review* 40: 1,397-432.

Poch, R.K. 1993. *Academic Freedom in American Higher Education: Rights, Responsibilities and Limitations.* ASHE-ERIC Higher Education Report No. 4. Washington, D.C.: Association for the Study of Higher Education. ED 366 263. 109 pp. MF-01; PC-05.

Pollard, D.S. 1990. "Black Women, Interpersonal Support, and Institutional Change." In *Changing Education: Women as Radicals and Conservators,* edited by J. Antler and S.K. Biklen. Albany: State University of New York Press.

Rabban, D.M. 1993. "A Functional Analysis of 'Individual' and 'Institutional' Academic Freedom Under the First Amendment." In *Freedom and Tenure in the Academy,* edited by W.W. Van Alstyne. Durham, N.C.: Duke University Press.

Reyes, M.D., and J.J. Halcon. 1988. "Racism in Academia: The Old Wolf Revisited." *Harvard Educational Review* 58(3): 299-314.

———. 1991. "Practices of the Academy: Barriers to Access for Chicano Academics." In *The Racial Crisis in American Higher Education,* edited by P.A. Altbach and K. Lomotey. Albany: State University of New York Press.

Roberts, S.V. Feb. 13, 1995. "Affirmative Action on the Edge." *U.S. News & World Report*: 32-38.

Rodriguez, R. 1982. *Hunger and Memory: The Education of Richard Rodriguez.* New York: Bantam Books.

Rothstein, L.F. 1991. "Students, Staff and Faculty Members With Disabilities: Current Issues for Colleges and Universities." *Journal of College and University Law* 17(4): 471-82.

School Law Reporter. December 1994. Topeka, Kan.: NOLPE.

Sowell, T. 1990. *Preferential Policies: An International Perspective.* New York: William Morrow & Co.

Steele, S. 1990. *The Content of Our Character: A New Vision of Race in America.* New York: St. Martin's Press.

Swan, P.N. 1990. "Subjective Hiring and Promotion Decisions in the Wake of Fort Worth, Antonio, and Price Waterhouse." *Journal of*

College and University Law 16(1): 553-72.

Tierney, W.G., and R.A. Rhoads. 1993. *Enhancing Promotion, Tenure and Beyond: Faculty Socialization as a Cultural Process.* ASHE-ERIC Higher Education Report No. 6. Washington, D.C.: Association for the Study of Higher Education. ED 368 322. 123 pp. MF-01; PC-05.

Trachtenberg, S.J. January/February 1996. "What Strategy Should We Now Adopt to Protect Academic Freedom?" *Academe* 82: 23-25.

Van Alstyne, W.W., ed. 1993a. *Freedom and Tenure in the Academy.* Durham, N.C.: Duke University Press.

———. 1993b. "Academic Freedom and the First Amendment in the Supreme Court of the United States: An Unhurried Historical Review." In *Freedom and Tenure in the Academy,* edited by W.W. Alstyne. Durham, N.C.: Duke University Press.

Wall Street Journal. Oct. 10, 1994. "Tenure: Many Will Decry It, Few Deny It." B1+.

Washington, V., and W. Harvey. 1989. *Affirmative Rhetoric, Negative Action: African-American and Hispanic Faculty at Predominantly White Institutions.* ASHE-ERIC Higher Education Report No. 2. Washington, D.C.: Association for the Study of Higher Education. ED 316 075. 128 pp. MF-01; PC-06.

Weeks, K.M. 1990. "The Peer Review Process: Confidentiality and Disclosure." *Journal of Higher Education* 61(2): 198-219.

West, C. 1993. *Race Matters.* Boston: Beacon Press.

Whicker, M.L., J.J. Kronenfeld, and R.A. Strickland. 1993. *Getting Tenure.* Survival Skills for Scholars 8. Newbury Park, Calif.: Sage Publications.

INDEX OF SUBJECTS

C

Calendra Italian American Institute, 116
California State University, 110
Centra, Nancy, xv
Chung vs. Park (1975), 21
City College of New York, 67
City of Richmond vs. J.A. Croson (1989), 113–114
City University of New York, 116
City University of New York Law School at Queens College, 24
Civil Rights Act of 1866, Section 1981, 93
Civil Rights Act of 1871, Section 1983, 93
Civil Rights Act of 1991, 89, 91
Claremont University, 87–88
Clark vs. Claremont University Center (1992), 87–88, 93
Cleveland State University 54, , 65
Coe vs. Board of Regents of the University of Wisconsin (1987), 29
Colburn vs. Trustees of Indiana University (1990), 51
Collective Bargaining, 32–41
collective bargaining
    at private institutions governed by Yeshiva decision, 39
    at public institutions governed by state law, 39
Commission on Academic Tenure in Higher Education, 3
committee deliberations and actual votes, access to, 130–132
Communist Party, issue of membership in, 64
"compelling need," requirement for disclosure of peer review
    confidential data , 124
"conditional tenure," judicial award of, 93
constitution
    definition of academic freedom, 9
    only matters of legitimate public concern protected under,
    65
    protection does not apply to faculty members at private
    institutions, 78
continuing violation doctrine, 80–81
contract law as basis for defining the rights of private institutions
    and their faculty, 9
contract of employment
    amendment of, 21–22
    language requiring use of race or gender preferences,
    115–116
C.W. Post Center of Long Island University (1971), 33
contractual rights may not be revoked by state law unless explicitly
    provided for, 24

Cooper vs. Ross (1979), 64
Craig vs. Alabama State University (1978), 88
criteria to provide guidance for re appointment, promotion, or
        tenure, 152–153

D

Davies, Ivor, 135
De factor tenure, 25–26, 47, 53–56
defamation
        allegations or other torts do not outweigh the right to
        privacy, 135
        definition of, 140–141
        liability and other claims against Peer-Review Evaluators,
        140–145
department and committee chairs liable for punitive damages, 85
Desimone vs. Skidmore College (1987), 131
Detroit Institute of Technology, 27
Dinnan, James, 123
        arrived at the jail dressed in full academic regalia, 132
"disability"
  recommendation that institutions adopt policies clearly defining
    and illegal discrimination in, 97
"discovery" information-gathering process, 120
discrimination
        based on physical disabilities, 96–97
        institutions should commit themselves to ending, 155–156
        most controversial awards for, 92
disparate-impact, 81-82, 88–92
disparate-treatment
        claim requires proof of intentional discrimination, 82
        definition, 81
Dixon vs. Rutgers (1987), 125
Dube, Ernest, 142–143
Dube vs. State University of New York (1990), 62, 142–143
due process rights, 46–47
Duquesne University, 40
Duquesne University (1982), 40

E

EEOC. See Equal Employment Opportunity Commission
Eleventh Amendment of the Constitution gives states immunity
        from lawsuits, 143
Employee right-to-know laws, 134–136

usually lose lawsuits, 149
fairness, institutions should treat faculty and be able to produce
        paper to show it, 157
Federal Rules of Evidence, 120, 127
        permit courts to issue protective orders against annoyance,
        132
financial exigency, court upheld dismissal of tenured faculty for, 6
First Amendment
        academic freedom as a "special concern of," 8
        can not be denied tenure or re appointment for exercise of,
        57
        faculty right to express themselves on matters of public
        concern, 66
        primacy over Title VII, 97
        right against disclosure of contested documents rejected by
        Supreme Court , 127
        right of institutional academic freedom recognized by
        Supreme Court, 121
        violations of rights under, 143
Fisher vs. Asheville-Buncombe Technical College (1993), 95
Florida Memorial College, 39
Ford vs. Nicks (1989), 81, 93
Fourteenth Amendment, 77. See also Equal Protection Clause of
        the 14th Amendment
        court held that scholarship for African-Americans violated,
        107
        does not give the guidance provided by detailed rules of
        federal law, 78
        rights, 46
        tenure rights protected under, 8
Frankfurter, Justice Felix, 58, 58–59
Franklin and Marshall College, 124, 131
freedom of learning, 58
Freedom of Speech and Academic Freedom, 57–58
freedom of teaching, 58
full disclosure, alternatives to, 132–133

G

Ganguli vs. University of Minnesota (1994), 23–24
"gatekeeper," need for with regard to tenure related papers
        requests," 155
gender-conscious hiring, upholding of affirmative-action plan
        calling for, 110

gender discrimination, legal basis for lawsuits against , 77

Goodman vs. Board of Trustees of Community College District 525 (1981), 115–116

contract language requires use of race or gender preferences, 115–116

Goodman vs. Gallerano (1985), 144, 144–145

Goodship, Joan, 95–96

Goodship vs. University of Richmond (1994), 95–96

Goss vs. San Jacinto Junior College (1979), 65–66

Goucher College, 6

Gray vs. Board of Higher Education, City of New York (1982), 131, 123

Greene vs. Howard University (1969), 9, 19

grievance procedures that are easy to use, institutions should establish, 157

Griggs vs. Duke Power Co. (1971), 89

grooming regulations, faculty need not abide by, 67

guidelines on elimination of tenured positions, 31

Gutzwiller vs. Fenik (1988), 84–85

H

Hackel vs. Vermont State colleges (1981), 35

Halpin vs. La Salle University (1994) , 18

Hander vs. San Jacinto Junior College (1975), 67

Harvard University, 124–125

Graduate School of Business, 82

Hill vs. Talledega College (1987), 17

Hispanic faculty members, percentage of full time, 102

homosexual, legal basis for appeal on discrimination against, 78

Honore vs. Douglas (1987), 27–28

Howard University, 9, 19, 141

Howard University vs. Best (1984), 141

I

Idaho State University, 22 , 50

incompetence, court upheld dismissal of tenured faculty for, 6

Inconsistent enforcement of procedures as a cause of faculty litigation, xiii

Indiana University, 51

informal practices, institutions should pay careful attention to, 150–151

information required by faculty members for tenure review, 152

Loyola University of Chicago, 21

M

Macalester College, 125

Managers

    as employees involved in developing and enforcing the
employer's policies, 36

    exclusion from labor laws, 36

mandatory-retirement programs, illegality of, 19

mandatory subjects under collective-bargaining agreement, 34–35

"manifest imbalance"

    proper criterion for proving, 110

    Equal Protection Clause probably would not permit an
argument based upon , 117

    Title VII affirmative-action cases more likely to succeed in
higher education, 114

"manifest racial imbalance" criteria, 108

Mansfield College, 21

Marwil vs. Baker (1980), 19

McCarthy era, caused expansion of legal basis of academic
freedom, 58

McDonnell Chair of East European History, 135

McDonnell Douglas Corp. vs. Green (1973), 82

    elements of a disparate-treatment claim outlined by Supreme
Court in, 82

McKee, 26

Meyer vs. Nebraska (1923), 58

Middle Tennessee State University, 81

Minor College, 31

misconduct, court upheld dismissal of tenured faculty for, 6

Moche vs. City University of New York (1992), 81

monetary damages, other comparable employment may be
required for, 81

Muhlenberg College, 83

Muskovitz vs. Lubbers (1990), 134

N

National Labor Relations Act of 1935, 33

National Labor Relations Board, 33.

    coverage, faculty as managerial or supervisory and thus
exempt from, 36–39

    decisions, conditions that seem to influence decisions of ,
40–41

jurisdiction, issue of religious institutions being subject to, 34

vs. Catholic Bishop of Chicago (1979), 34

vs. Florida Memorial College (1987), 39

vs. Stephens Institute (1980), 39

vs. Yeshiva University (1980), 36–39

National origin based discrimination, legal basis for lawsuits against, 77

Native American faculty members, percentage of full time, 102

Nazism, Apartheid, and Zionism as three forms of racism, teaching of, 62

neglect of duties, court upheld dismissal of tenured faculty for, 6

Neiman vs. Kingsborough Community College (1989), 34

New Jersey State College, 35

N.L.R.B. See National Labor Relations Board

notice of nonrenewal, faculty members require adequate, 32

O

Odessa Junior College, 47

"official immunity," 142

Ohio Public Records Act, 136

Olson vs. Idaho State University (1994), 22, 50, 56, 57

Omlor vs. Cleveland State University (1989), 54, 65

" on its face" claim. See prima facie claim

opinions usually are not considered defamatory because they cannot be "false," 141

oral promises not sufficient to create "property interests," 52

Orbovich vs. Macalester College (1988), 125

orientation and career development for faculty, institutions should provide, 153–154

outside jobs, faculty members can hold, 67

P

Palmer vs. District Board of Trustees of St. Petersburg Junior College (1984), 111

Parate vs. Isibor (1989), 63

Parnes, Rochelle, xv

part-time faculty members & adjunct professors, 1940 Statement does not apply to, 25

peer-review

evaluations, rationale for maintaining confidentiality of, 120–121

may need to prove position not within a "traditionally segregated job category," 110
Rhode Island School of Design, 20, 21, 54–55
Riggin vs. Board of Trustees of Ball State University (1986), 6
Right-to-know laws for employees, 134–136
Romer vs. Hobart and William Smith Colleges (1994), 23
Roos vs. Smith (1993), 66
Roth, David, 47–48
Rothstein (1991) recommends policies defining illegal "disability" discrimination, 97
Rutgers University, 35

S

Sam Houston State University, 144
same re appointment, promotion, and tenure policy should govern all units , 152
San Antonio Junior College, 47
San Jacinto Junior College 65-66, , 67
Scelsa vs. City University of New York (1992), 116
Scharf vs. Regents of the University of California (1991), 134–135
School of Allied Health Professions, 53
Scott vs. University of Delaware (1978), 76, 87
Section 1981 of the Civil Rights Act of 1866, 77
slander, definition of , 141
Snitow vs. Rutgers University (1986), 35–36
sociology defined as a "traditionally segregated" field, 110
Sola vs. Lafayette College (1986), 29, 116
Soni vs. Board of Trustees of the University of Tennessee (1975), 20, 27, 52
Southeastern Massachusetts University, 51
Stabelt vs. Smith (1989), 142–144
"staff planning document" exempt from disclosure requirements, 134
Stanford University, 135
State Ex Rel. James vs. Ohio State University (1994), 136–137
state law supersedes institutional authority with regard to tenure rights, 24
Statement of Principles on Academic Freedom and Tenure of 1940, 1, 7, 60
   does not apply to part-time faculty members and adjunct professors, 25
   as evidence of academic custom, 15

State sunshine laws, 136–138
State University of New York, 142–143
statistics, use in disparate-impact cases of, 89
Stephen F. Austin State University (1982), 142
Stephens Institute, 39
St. Petersburg Junior College, 111
"strict scrutiny"
      applies to affirmative action in public and not private
      institutions, 108
      constitutional standard of , 107
      test, requirement of, 113
student evaluations
      significant increase in the use for tenure decisions of, 5
      used by Peer-Review Committees, 138–140
subjective decision
      -making practices, can be attacked under disparate-impact
      theory, 89
      courts rarely question, 10
"sunshine laws," 133
Sunshine vs. Long Island University (1994), 81, 86–87
SUNY Stonybrook, 142
Sweezy, Paul, 58
Sweezy vs. New Hampshire (1957), 8, 58, 121

T

Talledega College 17, , 28
teaching portfolios, use of, 5
Tennessee State University, 63
tenure
      alternatives to, 2
      at public institutions, established by Supreme Court as a
      "property interest," 8
      benefits to institution of, 2
      by default, 26
      by grant, 25
      costs to institution of, 2
      court recognized methods of acquiring, 25
      "Density," 28–30
      determined by rules under which individual originally
      hired, 28
      did not exist in its present form before the 1940s, 6
      does not guarantee lifetime employment, 5–6

W

Washington vs. Davis (1976), 77

Waters vs. Churchill (1994), 67

Watson vs. Fort Worth Bank & Trust (1988), 89

Weber vs. Kaiser Aluminum Co. (1979), 108

Wharton School of Business, 126

white faculty

       employment - discrimination cases against historically black institutions, 74

       lawsuits against historically black institutions, 88

Whiting vs. Jackson State University (1980), 88

Wilde, Oscar, work in progress on, 85

William Smith Colleges, 23

Wirsing vs. Board of Regents of the University of Colorado (1990), 140

Wisconsin State University-Oshkosh, 47

women

       bringing cases against employment - discrimination, 74

       faculty members, percentage of full time, 102

Wygant vs. Jackson Board of Education (1986), 114

Y

Yeshiva University, 36–39

Z

Zimmerman vs. Minor College (1972), 31

ASHE-ERIC HIGHER EDUCATION REPORTS

Since 1983, the Association for the Study of Higher Education (ASHE) and the Educational Resources Information Center (ERIC) Clearinghouse on Higher Education, a sponsored project of the Graduate School of Education and Human Development at The George Washington University, have cosponsored the ASHE-ERIC Higher Education Report series. The 1995 series is the twenty-fourth overall and the seventh to be published by the Graduate School of Education and Human Development at The George Washington University.

Each monograph is the definitive analysis of a tough higher education problem, based on thorough research of pertinent literature and institutional experiences. Topics are identified by a national survey. Noted practitioners and scholars are then commissioned to write the reports, with experts providing critical reviews of each manuscript before publication.

Eight monographs (10 before 1985) in the ASHE-ERIC Higher Education Report series are published each year and are available on individual and subscription bases. To order, use the order form on the last page of this book.

Qualified persons interested in writing a monograph for the ASHE-ERIC Higher Education Reports are invited to submit a proposal to the National Advisory Board. As the pre-eminent literature review and issue analysis series in higher education, we can guarantee wide dissemination and national exposure for accepted candidates. Execution of a monograph requires at least a minimal familiarity with the ERIC database, including *Resources in Education* and current *Index to Journals in Education.* The objective of these reports is to bridge conventional wisdom with practical research. Prospective authors are strongly encouraged to call Dr. Fife at 800-773-3742.

For further information, write to
    ASHE-ERIC Higher Education Reports
    The George Washington University
    One Dupont Circle, Suite 630
    Washington, DC 20036
Or phone (202) 296-2597; toll free: 800-773-ERIC.
    Write or call for a complete catalog.

L. Jackson Newell
University of Utah

Steven G. Olswang
University Of Washington

James Rhem
The National Teaching & Learning Forum

Gary Rhoades
University of Arizona

G. Jeremiah Ryan
Harford Community College

Karl Schilling
Miami University

Charles Schroeder
University of Missouri

Lawrence A. Sherr
University of Kansas

Patricia A. Spencer
Riverside Community College

David Sweet
OERI, U.S. Department of Education

Barbara E. Taylor
Association of Governing Boards

Sheila L. Weiner
Board of Overseers of Harvard College

Wesley K. Willmer
Biola University

Manta Yorke
Liverpool John Moores University

REVIEW PANEL

Charles Adams
University of Massachusetts-Amherst

Louis Albert
American Association for Higher Education

Richard Alfred
University of Michigan

Henry Lee Allen
University of Rochester

Philip G. Altbach
Boston College

Marilyn J. Amey
University of Kansas

Kristine L. Anderson
Florida Atlantic University

Karen D. Arnold
Boston College

Robert J. Barak
Iowa State Board of Regents

Alan Bayer
Virginia Polytechnic Institute and State University

John P. Bean
Indiana University-Bloomington

John M. Braxton
Peabody College, Vanderbilt University

Ellen M. Brier
Tennessee State University

Barbara E. Brittingham
The University of Rhode Island

Dennis Brown
University of Kansas

Peter McE. Buchanan
Council for Advancement and Support of Education

Patricia Carter
University of Michigan

John A. Centra
Syracuse University

Arthur W. Chickering
George Mason University

Darrel A. Clowes
Virginia Polytechnic Institute and State University

Deborah M. DiCroce
Piedmont Virginia Community College

Cynthia S. Dickens
Mississippi State University

Sarah M. Dinham
University of Arizona

Kenneth A. Feldman
State University of New York-Stony Brook

Dorothy E. Finnegan
The College of William & Mary

Mildred Garcia
Montclair State College

Rodolfo Z. Garcia
Commission on Institutions of Higher Education

Kenneth C. Green
University of Southern California

James Hearn
University of Georgia

Edward R. Hines
Illinois State University

Deborah Hunter
University of Vermont

Philo Hutcheson
Georgia State University

Bruce Anthony Jones
University of Pittsburgh

Elizabeth A. Jones
The Pennsylvania State University

Kathryn Kretschmer
University of Kansas

Marsha V. Krotseng
State College and University Systems of West Virginia

George D. Kuh
Indiana University-Bloomington

Daniel T. Layzell
University of Wisconsin System

Patrick G. Love
Kent State University

Cheryl D. Lovell
State Higher Education Executive Officers

Meredith Jane Ludwig
American Association of State Colleges and Universities

Dewayne Matthews
Western Interstate Commission for Higher Education

Mantha V. Mehallis
Florida Atlantic University

Toby Milton
Essex Community College

James R. Mingle
State Higher Education Executive Officers

John A. Muffo
Virginia Polytechnic Institute and State University

L. Jackson Newell
Deep Springs College

James C. Palmer
Illinois State University

Robert A. Rhoads
The Pennsylvania State University

G. Jeremiah Ryan
Harford Community College

Mary Ann Danowitz Sagaria
The Ohio State University

Daryl G. Smith
The Claremont Graduate School

William G. Tierney
University of Southern California

Susan B. Twombly
University of Kansas

Robert A. Walhaus
University of Illinois-Chicago

Harold Wechsler
University of Rochester

Elizabeth J. Whitt
University of Illinois-Chicago

Michael J. Worth
The George Washington University

RECENT TITLES

1994 ASHE-ERIC Higher Education Reports

1. The Advisory Committee Advantage: Creating an Effective Strategy for Programmatic Improvement
   Lee Teitel

2. Collaborative Peer Review: The Role of Faculty in Improving College Teaching
   Larry Keig and Michael D. Waggoner

3. Prices, Productivity, and Investment: Assessing Financial Strategies in Higher Education
   Edward P. St. John

4. The Development Officer in Higher Education: Toward an Understanding of the Role
   Michael J. Worth and James W. Asp, II

5. The Promises and Pitfalls of Performance Indicators in Higher Education
   Gerald Gaither, Brian P. Nedwek, and John E. Neal

6. A New Alliance: Continuous Quality and Classroom Effectiveness
   Mimi Wolverton

7. Redesigning Higher Education: Producing Dramatic Gains in Student Learning
   Lion F. Gardiner

8. Student Learning Outside the Classroom: Transcending Artificial Boundaries
   George D. Kuh, Katie Branch Douglas, Jon P. Lund, and Jackie Ramin-Gyurnek

1993 ASHE-ERIC Higher Education Reports

1. The Department Chair: New Roles, Responsibilities, and Challenges
   Alan T. Seagren, John W. Creswell, and Daniel W. Wheeler

2. Sexual Harassment in Higher Education: From Conflict to Community
   Robert O. Riggs, Patricia H. Marred, and JoAnn C. Cutting

3. Chicanos in Higher Education: Issues and Dilemmas for the 21st Century
   Adalberto Aguirre Jr., and Ruben O. Martinez

4. Academic Freedom in American Higher Education: Rights, Responsibilities, and Limitations
   Robert K. Posh

5. Making Sense of the Dollars: The Costs and Uses of Faculty Compensation
   Kathryn M. Moore and Marilyn J. Amey

---

6. Enhancing Promotion, Tenure and Beyond: Faculty Socialization as a Cultural Process
   William C. Tierney and Robert A. Rhoads

7. New Perspectives for Student Affairs Professionals: Evolving Realities, Responsibilities, and Roles
   Peter H. Garland and Thomas W. Grace

8. Turning Teaching into Learning: The Role of Student Responsibility in the Collegiate Experience
   Todd M. Davis and Patricia Hillman Murrell

1992 ASHE-ERIC Higher Education Reports

1. The Leadership Compass: Values and Ethics in Higher Education
   John R. Wilcox and Susan L. Ebbs

2. Preparing for a Global Community: Achieving an International Perspective in Higher Education
   Sarah M. Pickert

3. Quality: Transforming Postsecondary Education
   Ellen Earle Chaffee and Lawrence A. Sherr

4. Faculty Job Satisfaction: Women and Minorities in Peril
   Martha Wingard Tack and Carol Logan Patitu

5. Reconciling Rights and Responsibilities of Colleges and Students: Offensive Speech, Assembly, Drug Testing, and Safety
   Annette Gibbs

6. Creating Distinctiveness: Lessons from Uncommon Colleges and Universities
   Barbara K. Townsend, L. Jackson Newell, and Michael D. Wiese

7. Instituting Enduring Innovations: Achieving Continuity of Change in Higher Education
   Barbara K. Curry

8. Crossing Pedagogical Oceans: International Teaching Assistants in U.S. Undergraduate Education
   Rosslyn M. Smith, Patricia Byrd, Gayle L. Nelson, Ralph Pat Barrett, and Janet C. Constantinides

1991 ASHE-ERIC Higher Education Reports

1. Active Learning: Creating Excitement in the Classroom
   Charles C. Bonwell and James A. Eison

2. Realizing Gender Equality in Higher Education: The Need to Integrate Work/Family Issues
   Nancy Hensel

3. Academic Advising for Student Success: A System of Shared Responsibility
    Susan H. Frost

4. Cooperative Learning: Increasing College Faculty Instructional Productivity
    David W. Johnson, Roger T. Johnson, and Karl A. Smith

5. High School-College Partnerships: Conceptual Models, Programs, and Issues
    Arthur Richard Greenberg

6. Meeting the Mandate: Renewing the College and Departmental Curriculum
    William Toombs and William Tierney

7. Faculty Collaboration: Enhancing the Quality of Scholarship and Teaching
    Ann E. Austin and Roger G. Baldwin

8. Strategies and Consequences: Managing the Costs in Higher Education
    John S. Waggaman

1990 ASHE-ERIC Higher Education Reports

1. The Campus Green: Fund Raising in Higher Education
    Barbara E. Brittingham and Thomas R. Pezzullo

2. The Emeritus Professor: Old Rank, New Meaning
    James E. Mauch, Jack W. Birch, and Jack Matthews

3. "High Risk" Students in Higher Education: Future Trends
    Dionne J. Jones and Betty Collier Watson

4. Budgeting for Higher Education at the State Level: Enigma, Paradox, and Ritual
    Daniel T. Layzell and Jan W. Lyddon

5. Proprietary Schools: Programs, Policies, and Prospects
    John B. Lee and Jamie P. Merisotis

6. College Choice: Understanding Student Enrollment Behavior
    Michael B. Paulsen

7. Pursuing Diversity: Recruiting College Minority Students
    Barbara Astone and Elsa Nuñez-Wormack

8. Social Consciousness and Career Awareness: Emerging Link in Higher Education
    John S. Swift Jr.

ORDER FORM

Quantity

95-1

Amount

_____ Please begin my subscription to the 1995 *ASHE-ERIC Higher Education Reports* at $98.00, 31% off the cover price, starting with Report 1, 1995. Includes shipping. _____

_____ Please send a complete set of the 1994 *ASHE-ERIC Higher Education Reports* at $98.00, 31% off the cover price. Please add shipping charge below. _____

Individual reports are available at the following prices:
1993, 1994 and 1995, $22.00; 1988-1992, $21.00; 1980-1987, $18.00

SHIPPING CHARGES
For orders of more than 50 books, please call for shipping information.

	1st three books	Ea. addl. book
U.S., 48 Contiguous States		
Ground:	$3.75	$0.15
2nd Day*:	8.25	1.10
Next Day*:	18.00	1.60
Alaska & Hawaii (2nd Day Only)*:	13.25	1.40

U.S. Territories and Foreign Countries: Please call for shipping information.
*Order will be shipped within 24 hours of a request.
All prices shown on this form are subject to change.

PLEASE SEND ME THE FOLLOWING REPORTS:

Quantity	Report No.	Year	Title	Amount

Please check one of the following:
☐ Check enclosed, payable to GWU-ERIC.
☐ Purchase order attached ($45.00 minimum).
☐ Charge my credit card indicated below:
  ☐ Visa ☐ MasterCard

Expiration Date_____

Subtotal: _____

Shipping: _____

Total Due: _____

Name_____

Title_____

Institution _____

Address_____

City _____ State _____ Zip_____

Phone _____ Fax _____Telex_____

Signature _____ Date_____

SEND ALL ORDERS TO: ASHE-ERIC Higher Education Reports
The George Washington University
One Dupont Cir., Ste. 630, Washington, DC 20036-1183
Phone: (202) 296-2597 • Toll-free: 800-773-ERIC